Kundalini

Expand Mind Power, Gain Spiritual Awareness, Open Your Third Eye, Enhance Psychic Abilities and Discover Transcendence

Lisa Blake

© Copyright 2020 by Lisa Blake. All right reserved.

The work contained herein has been produced with the intent to provide relevant knowledge and information on the topic on the topic described in the title for entertainment purposes only. While the author has gone to every extent to furnish up to date and true information, no claims can be made as to its accuracy or validity as the author has made no claims to be an expert on this topic. Notwithstanding, the reader is asked to do their own research and consult any subject matter experts they deem necessary to ensure the quality and accuracy of the material presented herein.

This statement is legally binding as deemed by the Committee of Publishers Association and the American Bar Association for the territory of the United States. Other jurisdictions may apply their own legal statutes. Any reproduction, transmission or copying of this material contained in this work without the express written consent of the copyright holder shall be deemed as a copyright violation as per the current legislation in force on the date of publishing and subsequent time thereafter. All additional works derived from this material may be claimed by the holder of this copyright.

The data, depictions, events, descriptions and all other information forthwith are considered to be true, fair and accurate unless the work is expressly described as a work of fiction. Regardless of the nature of this work, the Publisher is exempt from any responsibility of actions taken by the reader in conjunction with this work. The Publisher acknowledges that the reader acts of their own accord and releases the author and Publisher of any responsibility for the observance of tips, advice, counsel, strategies and techniques that may be offered in this volume.

TABLE OF CONTENTS

INTRODUCTION 1

Chapter 1 *What Is Mind Power?* 2

    The Kundalini Take on Mind Power 2

    The Power of Your Thoughts 3

    Exercising Your Creative Power 4

    Reality at a Thought-Level 5

Chapter 2 *A Clear Overview Of Physical Mind Power* 8

    Neuroplasticity and Neural Pathways 8

    Mental Stimulation for Improved Mind Power 9

    Physical Exercise and Dietary Considerations 10

    Maintaining a Healthy Bodily Function 11

    Caring for Your Emotional Wellbeing 12

Chapter 3 *A Mind-Expanding Diet* 14

    The Tridoshas 14

    The Types of Food 15

    Eating for Your Doshas 16

Chapter 4 *Yoga And Mind Power* 26

    The Snake in Your Spine 26

    White and Kundalini Yoga 26

    Tuning in for Your Session 27

    Kundalini Kriyas and Mantra 27

Chapter 5 *Relationships And Mind Power* 29

Creating Strong Relationships in Your Life 30

Using Relationships as a Point of Growth 32

How Relationships Affect Your Spiritual Energy 33

Chapter 6 *The Number One Mind Power Killer* **34**

The Secret Killer of Mind Power 34

How This Killer Affects Your Energy 35

How to Spot the Killer 35

What to Do About It 36

Protecting Yourself From It 38

Chapter 7 *The Mindset Aspects Of Mind Power* **39**

How Mindset Controls Your Mind Power 40

The Mindset That Unlocks Your Potential 40

Awakening Your Kundalini Mindsets 41

Incorporating a New Mindset Into Your Life 41

Chapter 8 *Having A Growth Mindset* **43**

Growth Mindset Vs. Fixed Mindset 43

Kundalini and Growth Mindset 44

Be Conscious About What You Feed Your Mind 44

Work on Your Desire 45

Have the Right Sources 45

Embrace a Drive to Learn 45

Stay Open and Flexible 46

Be Creative and Successful 46

Release Others' Influence Over You 46

Surround Yourself With Positivity 48

Speak of Present Success 48

Work Through Your Resistance 48

Chapter 9 *Deepening Your Sense Of Self* 50

Dissolution of Your Self 50

Substantiation of Your New Self 52

Exploring Life With Your New Identity 53

Expanding Your Perception of Self 54

Chapter 10 *Using Your Mind As A Problem Solver* 55

The Path of Ascended Problem Solving 55

Discovering a New Way for Everything 57

Becoming the Brightest Version of Yourself 57

Expanding Your Power to Others 58

Chapter 11 *Your Ego Needs Checking* 60

Shedding the Programmed Ego 61

Preventing Your Ego From Holding You Back 62

Creating an Egoless Future 63

Chapter 12 *Happiness Is Your Choice, Make It* 65

The Real Path to Happiness 65

How Happiness Improves Your Health 66

Consciously Choosing to Be Happy 66

Embracing a Lack of Happiness 67

Chapter 13 *How You Treat Them Is How You Treat You* 69

Why Your Intrapersonal Relationship Matters 69

Expanding the Quality of Your Relationship to Self 70

Unconditional Love and Acceptance of Others 72

Empowering All From Your Expanded Awareness 73

Chapter 14 *Becoming Your Biggest Cheerleader* 75

Feeling the Entirety of Your Presence 75

Celebrating Yourself on Every Level 76

Embracing Fearlessness In Your Life 76

Living as Your Authentic Self 77

Chapter 15 *Love Conquers All... Really* 78

Love to Overcome Ego 78

Unconditional Love Is the Goal 79

The Eightfold Theory of Love 79

Chapter 16 *Set Goals And Accomplish Them, Often* 82

The Achieve and Integrate Cycle 82

Setting Goals for Your Ascended Self 83

Reaching the Goals Energetically 83

Embodying Your Accomplishments 84

Chapter 17 *Create Healthy Habits* 86

Physically Embodying Healthy Habits 87

Healthy Habits for Your Limitless Mind 88

Caring for Your Emotions With Healthy Habits 88

Nurturing Your Spirit With Healthy Habits 89

Chapter 18 *Open Yourself Up To Change* 90

Embodying a Daily Kundalini Ritual 90

Opening Yourself Up to Change 91

Work With Change Intentionally 91

Being the Most Adaptable Version of Yourself 92

Chapter 19 *Exercise The Power Of Creativity* **94**

Creativity Is at the Root of Manifesting 94

Unlocking the Power of Your Creativity 95

Steps to Expand Your Creativity 96

Integrating Creativity Into Your Everyday Life 97

Conclusion **99**

Description **101**

INTRODUCTION

Welcome to *Kundalini*. You are about to tap into a significant wealth of knowledge that will allow you to tap fully into the power of your mind.

Each one of us has unlimited potential stored within the very power of our minds. This power enables us to achieve everything from basic day-to-day living to accomplishing extravagant, impressive, and life-changing goals that move us from the ordinary to the extraordinary. While every one of us can tap into this unlimited mind power, very few ever will. Some believe they are not lucky enough to have it, others believe it takes too much work, and others still are not convinced that mind power is real. You are not one of the many who will succumb to these weak thoughts, though. You are one of the strong ones, one of the ones who will take the necessary action to expand your mind power to achieve incredible things in life.

To help you tap into your unlimited potential in a comfortable, step-by-step way, I have defined everything you require to expand your mind power. From understanding what mind power is and where it resides to taking physical, mental, and emotional care of your mind, you will uncover every step required to help you reach your fullest potential. Believe it or not, it is not nearly as challenging as many make it out to be.

The most complicated part of activating your mind power is the element of consistency. Without consistency, nothing will ever stick. You must be willing to rise every day and take action on fueling your mind power if you desire to release yourself from the chains of mediocrity and create success in your life.

With adequate consistency, a hunger for change, and a willingness to do whatever it takes, you will discover there is nothing you cannot do in your life. If you are ready to expand your mind power and awaken the unlimited potential you already have within you, it is time to begin...

CHAPTER 1
What Is Mind Power?

Of all the powers you possess, mind power might be the most significant. Mindpower exists as the root power of everything you accomplish, become, and experience. Anytime you achieve anything in your life, regardless of how easy or complex it may have been to get there, you can be confident that you have tapped into mind power to get you there.

In Kundalini, mind power is achieved by awakening your energies and embodying them as profoundly as possible. The greater your mind power, the closer you are to enlightenment. People will spend their entire lives discovering how they can expand their mind power even further to achieve greater awakening levels.

Many people falsely believe mind power is inherent and that there is nothing you can do to expand or increase your mind power. These are the same people who believe that you achieve results through luck, and more often than not, they are not the "lucky type." Based on what Kundalini teaches, mind power can increase, strengthen, and be used to your advantage in many different ways. Whether you want to expand your business skills, increase your happiness, create better health, or design your dream lifestyle, all of this is achieved through mind power. Still, you might be wondering, what *is* mind power, exactly?

The Kundalini Take on Mind Power

To expand mind power, or to expand consciousness, is the ultimate goal of one's life. There are many practical and spiritual ways that you can identify and work with the energy of mind power, ranging from using your logical and rational brain in earthly matters to engaging in Kundalini yoga and meditation. Often, practitioners will adjust their entire lives to expand into their consciousness's depths. It is said that your mind power will continue to increase to the point that you achieve total enlightenment, at which point you have reached "maximum capacity."

Although mind power can drastically transform your physical life, many claim that the physical benefits of expanding your mind power no longer matter once you reach a significant point of expansion. While people who have experienced lower levels of enlightenment may believe that physical gains are the most remarkable thing about life, those who have experienced higher enlightenment levels are aware that material improvements are less enjoyable. The real enjoyment comes from the power you gain within yourself, and everything you can accomplish with that power, which is far beyond the physical world's fundamental limitations. Whether you want to bring the nonphysical into the material, invent something new, or experience the entirety of who you are, tapping into your unlimited mind power is a phenomenal way to do so.

The Power of Your Thoughts
To invent the light bulb, Thomas Edison first had to think about the value of harnessing the power of light. To develop the telephone, Alexander Graham Bell first had to think about the importance of communicating from great distances. To design the airplane, the Wright brothers first had to think about the importance of traveling through the air. Anytime something has been created or conceived in this world, whether it be magnificent or straightforward, it had first to be thought about, then it could be made. Without first bringing something into our awareness on a thought-level, there is no way to get into our realities on a physical level.

The impressive thing about thoughts is that, once you can think it, you can create it. Our minds are magnificently intelligent, and we possess an incredible capacity to turn any thought into our reality. Even if you cannot presently *see* how it might become your reality, your mind has everything required to pick apart this "problem" and turn your thoughts into your reality. Your thoughts are *the* most powerful thing you have in your life.

Think about it for a moment:

- The last time you were driving home and a detour on your usual route, you quickly resolved that problem by finding an alternate route home.
- When your boss had a challenge and needed you to resolve it, you rapidly thought about a creative solution to that problem.
- Every time you get home and prepare to make dinner, your mind rapidly solves "what to make?"
- The last time you got in an argument and decided you did not want to fight, your mind found a solution to help bring you peace.
- When you last came across an unexpected bill, your mind rapidly discovered a solution to help you pay for it.
- Every time you enter the grocery store with a mission to shop for everything on your list, your mind helps you do it efficiently.

Your mind is continually working to help you solve everyday problems and broader issues that may require more effort or more extensive solutions to get the results you need. Regardless of how small or large the question is or how long it takes you to find the answer, your mind *always* pulls through. As long as you give yourself enough time to focus and implement possible solutions, you find your way through any challenge you make.

This sheer mind power that gets you through everyday issues and more extensive problems you face in your life is the same mind power that invented everything in our modern world. No matter how significant or insignificant, every piece of technology was created through an individual's mind power that was willing to think of it, solve the problem, and bring it into our modern existence. Mindpower truly is the most significant power any one of us has.

Exercising Your Creative Power

The real fuel behind mind power is your creative power. Before you throw the breaks on this whole process and go, "Woah, woah, woah, I'm not creative at all. You should see my painting efforts. Stickmen look fancy compared to the junk I create!" I want to explain what I mean about creative power and emphasize that we all have creative control. Whether or not you can paint a Bob Ross-style painting or create an incredible mosaic table, you possess creative power within you that you tap into every single day. When you map out the quickest route to work each morning, you are harnessing your creative energy. When you wake up and decide what to make for breakfast, what order to get ready for work in, or how to spend your day off, you harness your creative energy. As you read this book and even envision yourself doing any of these things, you are harnessing your creative power. Every day, you are using your creative energy more than you can imagine, even if you are not using it intentionally, yet!

To make changes in your life, you must apply the power of creative thinking to create a new vision of what you want for yourself, and then you can work toward bringing that into your reality. Remember, you can imagine what you can experience, so as long as you can get it in at a thought level, you can create it in your real life.

The current video you are playing in your mind is one that tells you who you are, what you are capable of, what to think, and what to do in your life. By changing the video, you change your perspective, and you experience something more enjoyable in your life. It may seem strange or even unbelievable that change is this simple, but it is. The more you practice changing the video and witnessing something different in your mind, the more you will find yourself experiencing any transformation you desire in life. You begin to embrace the real power of manifesting, and you rapidly realize that you really *can* attract the life of your dreams, purely through the power of your creative thoughts.

Reality at a Thought-Level

Creating your reality from a thought-level is something you already do, naturally. There is no new skill that you need to discover or learn to harness this power and use it to your advantage. The real learning curve is discovering how you can become aware of this process to create your reality from a thought-level *intentionally*.

When you embrace Kundalini as a reality of life, the awakening you experience can alter your thought-patterns and ultimately shift the way you experience, and create, your truth. At first, you might experience chaos in your existence because of how chaotic and overwhelming Kundalini energy can be. As you find comfort in your awakening, you will discover that the mind power afforded to you by your continued awakening alters the way you experience reality and create yours.

I want you to think about the last time you were afraid of something and let fear win. You may have been afraid of your boss rejecting your request for a raise, people judging you for a choice you made, or you making a mistake with something you care much about. Regardless of the specific circumstances, I can almost guarantee that you spent time leading up to that scary event worrying and imagining your fear. You likely sat there, imagining the thing you were afraid of happening, happening. You visualized everything going wrong, you being rejected, shame or embarrassment growing, the catastrophic results of your failure, and every other possible detail you could. Perhaps you even imagined the conversations you would have or the excuses you would give when everything went wrong, and you inevitably screwed everything up.

When you reached the point where you could engage in the very thing that was making you fearful, things either went one of three ways:

- You chickened out.
- You did it and screwed everything up.
- You did it well enough and then suffered a "fear hangover."

Either way, you made the experience harder than it needed to be and capped your potential in that experience because you believed in the fear more than you believe in yourself.

To create a new reality from a thought-level, you need to harness this power you are already magnificent at and use it to your advantage. Using it effectively, you can stop yourself from chickening out and prevent poor or mediocre results by setting yourself up to reach your unlimited potential. Which by the way, your power is available in every moment, no matter how new you might be to something in your life. You do this by *changing the video.*

Change the video by envisioning something more empowering and giving yourself the chance to believe in *that* instead. Rather than thinking everything will go wrong, you will make a fool of yourself, or people will judge you, consider that everything will go right. Believe that your actions and attitude inspire people and that people have a *good* judgment of you, based on how you showed up. Imagine the things people will say to you to congratulate you on your win and the success speech you will share with people when they ask how you did it. By changing the tape, you uncap your potential.

CHAPTER 2
A Clear Overview Of Physical Mind Power

While your thoughts are where the magic happens, your mind power is not purely based on intangible ideas that you experience within your mind. Your brain's health plays a significant role in your control, as it provides you with the ability to have a healthy, well-functioning sense to provide you with your magnificent results in the first place. There are many ways that you can aid the physical wellness of your brain to improve your mind power, and it is suggested that you follow all of them. The stronger your brain is, the stronger your mind power can be, and the fewer limitations you have when it comes to uncapping your potential and creating your magical results.

Although Kundalini is a form of spiritual energy, it has a tangible impact on your physical body. One way that Kundalini affects your body is through affecting your brain, primarily through the creation of new neural pathways, as you begin perceiving and experiencing life in an entirely new way. It is tremendously helpful to discover how you can integrate Kundalini into your practical day to day life, allowing you to experience the energy in a grounded way. Although the goal is enlightenment, enlightenment is best achieved when you can remain grounded and firmly connected to current reality's physical powers.

Neuroplasticity and Neural Pathways

Thoughts are a seemingly magical experience that activates different parts of the brain and then disappears. Each opinion does not necessarily affect your mind, but thinking the same ideas over and over again can completely change your mind. The changes occur through what is known as neuroplasticity, or the brain's ability to create, modify, and maintain neural pathways.

When you experience a Kundalini awakening, your thought's behavior changes, which causes you to experience drastic transformations within your brain's wiring, old patterns that were seemingly hard-wired into your mind will fade to make way for new neural pathways to take place.

Improving your brain's neuroplasticity ensures that your brain has a physical advantage when improving your mind power. A brain with healthy neuroplasticity is one that has an easier time creating and sustaining neural pathways, which means you can introduce new neural pathways that can be used to your advantage. For example, if you want to develop the habit of exercising your body regularly so you can take better care of your physical health, a brain with excellent neuroplasticity will have an easier time creating neural pathways related to exercise habits. Keeping your mind's plasticity flexible and impressionable is not as simple as choosing your thoughts, as it requires far more generous support than that. By adequately supporting your brain through mental stimulation, physical exercise, diet, overall physical health, and emotional health, you maximize your neuroplasticity to ensure that learning and creating new things is more manageable. Thus, you genuinely uncap your mind power in a physical, practical manner.

Mental Stimulation for Improved Mind Power

To grow a muscle, you need to use it. If you want to grow your biceps, for example, you would curl weights and gradually increase those weights until you have more muscular biceps. Then, you would continue curling those weights to maintain that strength. The same goes for your brain. If you want to improve your mind power, you need first to use the mind power you already have, then challenge it so that it is encouraged to grow stronger and healthier. As you continue stimulating your mind, you continue experiencing greater mind power.

There are many mentally stimulating activities you can engage in that will improve your neuroplasticity and support you with healthily creating new neural pathways. Reading, learning further information or skills, completing puzzles, using mental math, experimenting, and even using your physical body in new or unexpected ways are great opportunities to improve your neuroplasticity and increase your mind power. You must incorporate these mentally stimulating activities into your day-to-day life as often as possible, as this enables you to continuously expand your mind power. Anytime you are doing a regular daily activity, do not be afraid to do it differently, add a new skill into the mix, or unusually move your body as you do it. This unusual movement forces your brain to become more active and increases your mental flexibility around said activity, which increases your neuroplasticity and learning abilities.

Another excellent form of the mental stimulation you can engage in is Kundalini yoga or Kundalini meditation. These activities will trigger Kundalini energy to begin awakening and rising through your body and soul, which affects your entire system, including your mind. With yoga, you are priming your mind through low-impact routines that activate various forms of energy within you and create shifts within your body and mind. Meditation encourages you to use your brain in a focused, intentional manner that activates various powers while also working on your physical mind. Though both of these may seem unassuming, they have a tremendous impact on your brain's wellbeing and should be engaged with consistently.

Physical Exercise and Dietary Considerations

You are taking adequate care of your physical body aids in promoting healthy, balanced hormone levels. When your hormones are balanced, your brain has the optimal conditions for maintaining neuroplasticity and cultivating new neural pathways. Brains inundated with excess stress levels, or that lack of certain excess hormones, are less likely to function as they ought to. Inappropriate hormone levels, such as those associated with stress or other intense emotions, trigger the brain to behave differently from it normally, causing a lack of neuroplasticity or difficulty developing new neural pathways. Adequate physical exercise and a proper, healthy diet ensure that you are likely to experience optimal health, which means you experience balanced hormones that function correctly within your body.

Another benefit of physical exercise is that it not only levels out unwanted hormones and chemicals within your body but also promotes the development of hormones and chemicals that improve mental clarity and cognitive function. You should seek to get at least 30 minutes of exercise daily, while also opting to stay in motion throughout the day. Walk or bike rather than drive, take the stairs, stretch as often as you can, and spend as much time in motion as possible. If you cannot be in action, hold a robust and healthy posture, so your body thrives. Through all of this, you minimize stress and promote good health within your body, creating room for a robust and healthy brain function.

Your diet can help regulate hormones while also introducing essential nutrients to your body, which promotes good brain health. For your brain, specifically, Omega-3 fatty acids, folate, vitamin E, and flavonoids are all excellent for brain health. You can get these nutrients through nuts, fish, dark leafy greens, berries, teas, and avocados. Through these, your brain has the most effortless ability to maintain neuroplasticity and to develop new neural pathways as they are needed. With foods, just like some are beneficial, some can be harmful. Refined sugars and fats, trans fats, highly processed foods, aspartame, alcohol, and fish high in mercury can harm brain health. Avoiding all of these, while also eating more of the healthy nutrients, can improve your overall brain health so you can tap into unlimited levels of mind power. Through this, your mind truly thrives!

In ancient East Indian tradition, which Kundalini stems from, the diet was a significant factor in spiritual well being. Ayurveda, which means "The Science of Life," is a science of nutritional medicine that enabled people to balance their physical bodies to match their spiritual enlightenment. By physically treating your body with nutrition, you can adjust your earthly energy to reach your awakening soul's powers. You could also improve your soul's awakening abilities by offering it the tangible powers it needs to unite between the physical and spiritual realms.

Maintaining a Healthy Bodily Function

Focusing specifically on brain health is a natural tendency when we are discussing mind power, but it is essential to realize those other aspects of your health play into your brain's health, too. The easiest way to understand this is to recognize that your whole body is suffering anytime one part of your body is unhealthy. When you experience ill health even in one small area of your body, your brain increases your stress hormones to give your body adequate energy to correct it. Suppose you continue to experience that ailment by failing to improve your health. In that case, you continue to experience elevated stress hormones that affect your brain and the rest of your body.

Keep your blood pressure and blood sugars healthy, ensure you look after your gut health, maintain your skin health, and otherwise look after your health to maintain optimal wellbeing. Creating optimal wellbeing throughout your entire body by respecting your system as a whole ensures that your overall wellness will be strong enough to boost your mind power and keep you healthy.

Kundalini yoga is an incredible way to maintain healthy bodily function, as each pose is designed to improve the flow of energy through your body. Modern studies have shown that engaging in yoga consistently improves physical strength and the health of your hormones, muscles, joints, tendons, circulatory system, metabolism, and virtually all other processes in your body. Engaging in Kundalini yoga at least five days per week is an excellent way to reap in these benefits, while also activating your Kundalini to expand your mind power.

When engaging Kundalini yoga, it is a good idea to work alongside a trained instructor. At least, initially, Kundalini yoga is intense and triggers strong awakenings, which can be overwhelming if you are unaware of what to expect. An adequately trained instructor can help guide you through the poses and the awakening that follows, as well as any energetic experiences you might have during the process. This is highly beneficial in allowing you to enjoy your awakening healthily and powerfully to improve your experience overall.

Caring for Your Emotional Wellbeing

Beyond physical considerations, you also need to care for your emotional wellbeing. Emotions are responsible for creating various hormones and chemicals in your body, such as cortisol, dopamine, serotonin, endorphins, oxytocin, and adrenaline. If your emotions remain unchecked, your body will continue to create these hormones and chemicals, leading to you experiencing them at unhealthy levels.

Caring for your emotional wellbeing ensures that you gain relief from your triggers, which means these hormones and chemicals stop being produced in excess levels. You can return to a basic level of calm once again. You can care for your emotional well-being by being compassionate and accepting of your emotions, talking to a therapist or venting with a trusted friend, journaling, and healthily expressing yourself. You can also care for your emotional wellbeing by making choices that do not stimulate unwanted personal experiences or thinking before you act. Managing your stress and striving for balance in advance is a great way to ensure that you do not end up experiencing an excess of unexpected and unwanted emotions later on.

Those who actively work toward their enlightenment recognize that there is no such thing as "you" or "I." Instead, there is only a "we." Thus, if someone were to neglect their wellbeing, they would be expressing an apparent lack of concern for others' wellbeing. Spending time caring for your physical, mental, and emotional health ensures that you are taking proper care of your Self so that you can express the same level of care and concern for others. This increases your capacity to experience and give love. Thus, you learn to love yourself and others more.

CHAPTER 3
A Mind-Expanding Diet

You may have caught the introduction of Ayurveda in the previous chapter, which is a topic that is essential to any discussion regarding Kundalini and mind power. According to the ancient Hindu peoples, you cannot have one without the other, so you must learn to support yourself through Ayurveda if you also wish to support yourself through Kundalini.

Ayurveda discusses topics relating to food and nutrition and recognizes them as tangible, practical ways to support our wellbeing. Hindu peoples see food as a spiritual experience, as you are assimilating your food's energy to your body, which can be either a benefit or a hindrance depending on what you are consuming. In Ayurveda, they fail to recognize a "one-size-fits-all" approach. Instead, there are three primary guidelines to follow based on your dominant dosha.

The Tridoshas

The tridoshas represent the three doshas that we each experience in our lives and bodies. The first dosha is Vata, which represents air. The second dosha is Pitta, which represents bile. The third dosha is Kapha, which represents phlegm. All three aspects of the physical self are relevant to your spiritual well being, and the metabolic processes of your body, which is why they are included in the doshas. Though the tridoshas represent aspects of the metabolic system, they are recognized as being doshas within themselves, which are life forces.

The Vata dosha is known for containing air and ether properties, and it is responsible for your energy levels. Vata also affects your movement and nerve impulses, which means breath, circulation, speech, and digestion are manifestations of the Vata dosha. If you have a Vata-dominant dosha, you are a light, enthusiastic, and creative individual. You likely have a quick-wit, and you are open to trying new experiences, especially if it means you get to stay active since you quite enjoy moving around. As a Vata-dominant, you are flexible and easy to be around, but can also be highly forgetful.

The Pitta-dominant dosha represents a well-structured person that can concentrate well and is exceptional with project management. They are always focused on practicality and leadership and love to work as teachers or guides because this allows them to spend time in their natural element. Pitta-dominant types can be more prudent with their money and other resources, as they are practical and logical in everything they do. Despite being pragmatic and focused, the Pitta type still mostly enjoys the outdoors and appreciates getting to spend energy in nature. Because of their Type-A personalities, Pitta-dominant people can be fiery and even aggressive because of the rage they often hold inside of them.

The Kapha-dominant dosha can be seen in people that are balanced, humble, and grounded. They are patient and understanding and work excellently in managerial roles to guide people without becoming overwhelmed or hot-headed by different experiences. Kapha-dominant types are also excellent with their memory and can often remember even the most minor and seemingly insignificant details of anything they experience. Routine and regularity are essential to a Kapha-dominant person, but they can lean toward habits of overeating, over-sleeping, and insufficient exercise if they are not careful.

The Types of Food

In Ayurveda, there are three types of food that you should know about: sun foods, ground foods, and earth foods. These foods provide you with different benefits, so you must regularly eat from all three categories. However, the amount you eat from each type will vary depending on which of your doshas is most dominant. Generally speaking, you want to eat fewer foods associated with your dominant dosha and more foods related to your less dominant doshas, especially favoring your least dominant dosha overall. This way, you balance your physical energy to your spiritual life, which is believed to help your enlightenment.

Sun foods are any foods that grow well above the ground, such as fruits. Eating plenty of fruits will give you the bright, fiery energy of the sun, which helps liven up your personal power and bring you closer to enlightenment.

Ground foods grow close to the ground, such as grains, vegetables, and low-growing fruits like strawberries. Ground foods are excellent for cleansing your body and energy and keeping you grounded in your Self and Spirit.

Earth foods are those that grow beneath the ground, such as root vegetables. Consuming earth foods is excellent for helping heal your body and energy, so consume them regularly. It is always a good idea to consume a wide range of colors when you eat the sun, ground, and earth foods to ensure that you are getting the best energy intake possible, so eat the rainbow!

Eating for Your Doshas

Eating for your dosha depends on which dosha is your dominant one. You can identify your dominant dosha by taking a simple Ayurveda test online, which will allow you to discover which of your doshas is most prevalent and which is least. From there, you can eat your diet accordingly to help balance your dominant dosha and elevate your least dominant one.

If you have a Vata-dominant dosha, you must eat cooked vegetables, well-ripened fruits, dairy, small amounts of poultry or seafood, sweeteners, and grains. It is important to avoid using spices in large quantities and avoid bitter and astringent herbs, as they will not work well with your dosha type.

Vata-dominant doshas should eat:

- Almonds
- Apricots

- Asparagus
- Avocados
- Bananas
- Beets
- Berries
- Carrots
- Chicken
- Chickpeas
- Cherries
- Coconut
- Cucumber
- Dairy (all)
- Figs
- Garlic
- Ghee
- Grapefruit
- Grapes
- Green beans
- Lemons
- Mangoes
- Mung beans
- Olive oil
- Onions
- Papaya
- Peaches
- Pineapple
- Pink lentils
- Plums
- Seafood
- Sesame oil
- Sour oranges

- Stewed fruits
- Sweet melons
- Sweet potatoes
- Radishes
- Tofu
- Turkey
- Turnips

In moderation, Vata-dominant types can eat:

- Barely
- Black beans
- Broccoli
- Brussels sprouts
- Buckwheat
- Cabbage
- Cauliflower
- Celery
- Corn
- Cranberries
- Eggplant
- Kidney beans
- Leafy green vegetables
- Millet
- Mushrooms
- Peas
- Pears
- Peppers
- Pomegranates
- Potatoes

- Red meat
- Sprouts
- Tomatoes
- Wheat
- Zucchini

Vata-dominant types should avoid eating:

- Astringent herbs and spices
- Bitter herbs and spices
- Dried fruits
- Unripe fruits

If you have a Pitta-dominant dosha, anything that has a bitter, sweet, or astringent taste is best, as well as cold or warm foods. Because your dosha indicates that you are fiery and passionate, it makes sense that you need cooler foods to help you balance your fire energy.

Pitta-dominant doshas should eat:

- Asparagus
- Avocado
- Bananas
- Barley
- Broccoli
- Brussels sprouts
- Butter
- Cabbage
- Carrots
- Cauliflower
- Celery
- Cherries

- Chicken
- Chickpeas
- Coconut
- Cucumber
- Egg whites
- Figs
- Flaxseeds
- Ghee
- Grapeseed oil
- Green beans
- Green peppers
- Leafy green vegetables
- Lettuce
- Mangoes
- Melons
- Milk
- Mung beans
- Mushrooms
- Oats
- Okra
- Olive oil
- Oranges
- Parsley
- Pears
- Peas
- Pineapples
- Plums
- Potatoes
- Prunes
- Pumpkin seeds
- Radishes

- Raisins
- Red lentils
- River fish
- Shrimp
- Spinach
- Sprouts
- Squash
- Sunflower oil
- Sunflower seeds
- Sweet potatoes
- Tofu
- Turkey
- Wheat
- White rice
- Zucchini

In moderation, Pitta-dominant types can eat:

- Almond oil
- Apricot
- Apples
- Ar har Dal
- Beets
- Berries
- Black gram
- Black lentils
- Brown rice
- Cheese
- Chiles
- Coconut oil
- Corn

- Corn oil
- Dark grapes
- Eggplants
- Egg yolk
- Grapefruit
- Hot peppers
- Ice cream
- Millet
- Onions
- Peaches
- Persimmons
- Pineapples
- Raw papaya
- Red meat
- Rye
- Safflower oil
- Seafood
- Sesame oil
- Sour buttermilk
- Sour cherries
- Sour cream
- Sour yogurt
- Tomatoes

Pitta-dominant types should avoid eating:

- Fermented foods
- Honey
- Molasses
- Spices

If you have a Kapha-dominant dosha, you must favor warm, light, and dry foods. Lightly cooked meals are excellent, too, though you should select eating as much raw food as possible to balance your energy. Spicy food is ideal for Kapha-dominant doshas, also, so enjoy as much spicy food as you want!

Kapha-dominant doshas should eat:

- Almond oil
- Apples
- Apricots
- Asparagus
- Barley
- Basmati rice
- Beans (all types)
- Beets
- Berries
- Broccoli
- Brussels sprouts
- Buckwheat
- Cabbage
- Camel milk
- Carrots
- Cauliflower
- Celery
- Cherries
- Chicken
- Corn
- Cranberries
- Dried fruits
- Eggs

- Eggplant
- Flaxseeds
- Garlic
- Goats milk
- Grapefruits
- Grapeseed oil
- Leafy green vegetables
- Lean fish
- Lettuce
- Millet
- Mushrooms
- Oats
- Okra
- Olive oil
- Onions
- Papaya
- Pears
- Peas
- Peppers
- Pomegranate
- Potatoes
- Prunes
- Pumpkin seeds
- Radishes
- Rye
- Skim milk
- Soy milk
- Spices (all)
- Spinach
- Sprouts
- Sunflower oil

- Sunflower seeds
- Turkey

In moderation, Kapha-dominant types can eat:

- Bananas
- Coconuts
- Cucumbers
- Dates
- Egg yolks
- Fresh figs
- Kidney beans
- Mangoes
- Red meat
- Rice
- Shrimp
- Sweet potatoes
- Tofu
- Tomatoes
- Wheat
- Zucchini

Kapha-dominant types should avoid eating:

- Hot cereals
- Steamed grains

CHAPTER 4
Yoga And Mind Power

Kundalini yoga is one of the primary ways to connect to spirit, activate your life force energy, and trigger your enlightenment. From the outside, Kundalini yoga looks like a series of exercises and postures to move the physical body. However, the reality of what is going on lies far more profound than mere physical movements. When engaged in Kundalini yoga, you are also involved in deep meditation, which allows you to activate your energy and awaken your Kundalini. Yoga will both facilitate the awakening and guide you through balancing and relaxing your awakened powers. This is the optimal way to integrate your life for a deeper connection to higher self and consciousness.

The Snake in Your Spine

In Kundalini, it is said that your life force energy coils around your spine and, upon activating, "slithers" up your spine and out your crown chakra like a snake uncoiling and slithering away from a branch. When you activate your energy, you are likely to see and feel this energy moving up through your body and awakening each of your chakras along the way.

Even after your initial awakening, you will continue to experience imagery and energy as your life force energy routinely uncoils and awakens even further, and moves through your chakras with greater consistency. Throughout your day to day life, your Kundalini energy will gradually relax back into the base of your spine, so regular yoga practices are essential to release this energy and promote healing and awakening.

White and Kundalini Yoga

Kundalini yoga classes are chock full of people wearing white. Wearing white is essential, as colors are said to create an uncontrollable action within your subconscious mind, which affects your productivity, inspiration, and expansion. Since you want to be deeply engaged in your session, you do not wish to have the distracting effects of colors taking away from your experience, which is why practitioners commonly wear white.

Tuning in for Your Session

Before every session, you must start by tuning in. Tuning in allows you to become aware of your energy, connect to your higher self, and connect to higher powers. To clear and neutralize your mind means to release the five causes of unhappiness: lust, anger, greed, pride, and attachment. When you remove these from your consciousness and deeply tune into your energy field, you gain the ability to experience more peace and harmony in all areas of your life.

Tuning in is achieved by chanting *Ong Namo Guru Dev Namo* as you remain seated with your hands over your heart center in prayer pose. This mantra translates to "bowing to the truth within you; your relationship to your own destiny."

Kundalini Kriyas and Mantra

Once you are tuned in, you can commence your Kundalini yoga session with Kriyas and mantras. Kriyas are the practices you will follow, while mantras incite Kundalini yoga's meditation aspect so you can achieve higher consciousness through your session. In this way, you unite your physical and spiritual elements to create a whole-body experience.
The kriyas you fulfill will be done from a seated position. Start by extending your arms above your head and shaking them, as well as your entire upper body and your head. This shaking releases fear, anxiety, and other pent-up emotions from your body so you can experience freedom from the tension and overwhelm.

Next, you can move into a shoulder stand. If you are capable, a shoulder stand can be accomplished by rolling up through your spine and straightening your legs straight above you as you lean upon your shoulders. If you can do this properly and maintain it, it is said that a 15-minute shoulder stand is the equivalent of sleeping for 2 hours.
Seated rock pose is an excellent Kundalini kriya to use. You can enter this pose by sitting with your shins tucked under you. Then, bring your hands to your shoulders with your

elbows out wide and keep your spine straight and tall. Inhale, then turn to the left, exhale and turn to the right. Your spine should remain in the same place vertically, though it should be rotating left and right with each inhale and exhale.

Deep squats can be done by keeping your hands at your heart in prayer pose. You should keep your spine straight and tall, too. Bend at your knees, dropping your bottom toward the ground, but keep your head upright. As you lower, inhale, and as you come back up, exhale.

Finally, spinal flexion is a great move that can be achieved by sitting in a cross-legged position. You want to move your chest forward but keep your head still, then move your chest backward while still keeping your head in the same place. Your arms should be moving with you as you move back and forth. This helps open your diaphragm and chest, as well as your shoulders.

The mantra you can say as you engage in Kundalini yoga practice is "Sa Ta Na Ma." These sounds represent the universe's five primal sounds: infinity, life, death and transformation, and rebirth. Chant them to yourself following your kriyas to activate these energies within your being and expand your mind power.

CHAPTER 5
Relationships And Mind Power

If you truly want to unlock any power within yourself, it pays to spend time researching historical humans and the way we once were. Understanding our species' history allows you to understand the nature of who you are, which enables you to tap into the power of instinct and primal urges. Historically speaking, humans have always been a tribal species, meaning we thrive with connection and being close to others of our own kind. We also thrive when we have interspecies relationships, such as the ones we share with our dogs, cats, and other beloved family pets. However, relationships with our own kind are optimal as they enable us to feel received, connected, safe, and accepted by our own kind. They are indeed essential to our wellbeing.

Beyond the physical benefits you gain from thriving relationships, it has also been shown that you gain extensive value spiritually. Your relationships add energy to your life and can impact your power, too. When you engage in high-quality, thriving relationships with people who support you with elevating your energy and wellbeing, you further awaken your own energy field and increase your enlightenment. The people we surround ourselves by can heavily encourage us, causing us to take our own enlightenment more seriously, too, which can inspire you to work more persistently toward activating the entirety of your mind power.

Extensive evidence from modern research has shown that humans thrive on high-quality relationships with other humans, as they allow us to live longer, happier lives. Those who have healthy relationships with other humans are known for having fewer mental health problems because their brains are functioning in the best possible manner. When you have close, positive relationships with others, you gain a sense of purpose and find yourself feeling as though you belong, all of which have a positive impact on your brain's health, and therefore your mind power.

Loneliness and isolation are two conditions that have grown in the technology era, mainly because people are primarily nurturing relationships behind screens rather than face to face. Though it does create a sense of connection, it is not the same as the one you experience when you are in physical contact with someone, or at the very least, when you can see them face to face. As humans, we have something called a mirror neuron, which is responsible for us feeling close and connected with other humans. Essentially, when we behave in some way or observe someone else acting somehow, the mirror neuron is enabled, and we begin to recognize similarities between ourselves and others. Those similarities lead to empathy, compassion, deeper bonds, and a meaningful sense of belonging. When we do not spend enough time around other people, our neurons do not fire, and we fail that tangible sense of connection with others.

The other side of this is that, when we fail to have healthy relationships with others, we fail to feel a sense of belonging, which leads to less real psychological issues that are still just as serious. Reduced self-esteem, a lack of self-confidence, and disorders such as anxiety, depression, and even individual personality disorders can all be triggered when we feel as though we do not belong with our "tribe." If you truly want to tap into your unlimited mind power, you must focus on nurturing healthy, positive relationships in your life.

Creating Strong Relationships in Your Life

Creating healthy relationships in your life is something we are all intended to learn as children, but it doesn't always go as planned. Learning how to build healthy, stable relationships in adulthood takes practice. Still, it can become a skill that you are strong with, which means it becomes easier for you to create and enjoy healthy relationships with fellow adults.

There are five significant steps you can take toward developing strong relationships in your life: give time, be present, listen, be listened to, and recognize unhealthy relationships.

Giving time to your relationships is one of the most powerful things you can do, though it might feel impossible if your schedule is continually packed with things to do. You might find that you are so invested in your career and your family that making time for your friends seems challenging, so it becomes a low priority. You must realize the importance of these relationships and commit time to them, even when it seems challenging, so that you can invest in your relationships in a healthy manner.

Being present is an essential step to building relationships, as it allows you to ensure that you are entirely in the moment with those you are spending time with. When you do carve out time for your friends or family, be sure that you are entirely available and that you are enjoying that time with them. Put your phone away, stop giving mental energy to issues you are dealing with elsewhere, and allow yourself to become fully present in that moment. Enjoy the time you are spending with your loved ones, as this presence massively deepens the connection you share by having each of you invested in developing your relationship with each other, rather than with distractions.

Listening is one of the best things you can do when nurturing relationships, especially as an adult. As children, we do not worry about listening to our peers because we are all so preoccupied with our own experiences. As adults, we thrive when those around us hear us. Listen to what your friends are saying in a non-judgmental way, and concentrate on their needs when they are talking. Allow yourself to truly hear about your friends, who they are, and what they are experiencing, and witness how this deepens your bond as you come to understand your friend even more.

Being listened to is another valuable asset to any budding relationship. You might feel as though you should hold things in, hide certain aspects of your personality, or otherwise contour who you are to meet the needs of someone else. Especially in adulthood, relationships, where such nonsense is expected, should not be maintained. Be honest, authentic, and clear; allow others to receive you and support you as you are. This shows those you are sharing a relationship with that you are also willing to be open, which allows them to feel comfortable opening up around you.

Lastly, you need to be able to recognize and eliminate unhealthy relationships from your life. Relationships where you are always listening, always talking, people are manipulating you, negativity or drama seeps in, or other toxic behaviors are ruling should always be eliminated. You can be seriously affected mentally, emotionally, and even physically when you are in unhealthy relationships, as they are incredibly harmful. Recognizing the harm of these situations can help you move forward healthily by either resolving the toxicity in the relationship or dissolving the relationship altogether.

Using Relationships as a Point of Growth

Beyond offering you a chance to bond with others and experience a deepened sense of belonging and connection, relationships can offer many impressive points of growth. The increase you feel in your personal value and self-confidence and self-esteem will have a significant impact on your wellbeing; however, you can become even more intentional inside your relationships to use them as a significant growing point in your life.

One excellent way relationships help you grow is by increasing your sense of trust in yourself. When you realize that you are an emotionally dependable person and capable of adding value to other people's lives, it allows you to see yourself as a positive, wholesome individual. When you realize that you can support others, you stop feeling timid in relationships and your life because you know you can benefit yourself, and others, in a positive manner.

Another great way to intentionally grow through your relationships is to use them to learn about yourself and use them as an opportunity to learn in general. To learn about yourself, relationships offer you the ability to understand how you relate to others and what you need in a relationship to feel valued and supported. You also learn about how you can behave in a healthier manner inside of relationships by recognizing how you can support others with having their needs met and how you can have your needs met inside each relationship. It can be incredibly powerful to understand the role friendship plays versus the role an acquaintanceship or romantic relationship plays in your life and to discover how to fulfill your needs and the needs of others within each relationship. Through this, you effectively increase your independence while also improving the level of connection you share with others, which creates an excellent learning opportunity.

When it comes to learning from others directly, relationships of all varieties can provide you with the opportunity to see things from different perspectives. As you get to know your friends, acquaintances, or romantic partners, you get to know what their points of view are on the world, and how these may influence you to grow your point of view. This expanding point of view may help you with personal issues, or it may allow you to understand others better so you can deepen your compassion and expand the value of your relationships. Either way, you will be developing your mind power as your cup overflows with support, understanding, knowledge, and experience.

How Relationships Affect Your Spiritual Energy

Relationships can either add to or take away from your wellbeing. Even seemingly neutral relationships will either add or take away, depending on where they fall on the benefits spectrum. When you are in negative relationships, it shows how your energy feels and how you show up in life. Negative associations will drain your energy, negatively influence you, and leave you feeling as though you are continually adjusting yourself or cleansing your energy field from chaos. The more you experience these types of drama and chaos in your relationships, the more you find yourself struggling to support your enlightenment because you are getting caught up with too much "yuck" on earth.

Positive relationships, on the other hand, can drastically improve the quality of your life. When you are surrounded by people that take their energy seriously, work toward their enlightenment, and routinely improve upon themselves, you can feel it. You feel empowered and uplifted when you are around them, can enjoy greater feelings of growth, and you are motivated to stay on track with your personal development. These positive relationships are beneficial, making you far more likely to enjoy your awakening and feel balanced and empowered in your life.

CHAPTER 6
The Number One Mind Power Killer

If you truly want to transform your life's quality and expand your mind power beyond your wildest beliefs, you *must* eliminate the number one mind power killer from your life. This killer often lurks in the shadows, silently sneaking in and finding ways to decimate your sense of confidence and wellbeing. It will destroy your mind power and your physical wellbeing, and the quality of your life as a whole.

The trouble with this killer is that every one of us faces it, as it is a natural part of life. In fact, in small doses and under control, the killer is actually an assistant and can support you in many different ways. However, most people experience out-of-control relationships with this killer, which is why it has the capacity to become so toxic and destroy the wellbeing of so many.

The Secret Killer of Mind Power...

The secret killer of mind power is lurking in your everyday life. You experience it frequently, likely even daily. If you are ahead of the game, you have already found a way to identify and stop the killer in its tracks, but if you are not, you are likely still struggling with it regularly. You experience the killer anytime you receive unexpected news, your boss tightens a deadline on a project you were already late for, your to-do list gets too long, or you have to do something you do not want to do. The secret killer of mind power is also known as *stress*.

When it is in balance, stress gives you that little boost of energy you need to get things done. Stress can be helpful in the immediate moment, or as a short-term motivator that supplies the energy and mental focus you need to achieve anything you desire. When it isn't in balance, or you experience it for a prolonged period of time, stress creates more problems than it solves. Over time, your heightened focus becomes anxiety, excess energy becomes problematic, and emotional pressure begins to feel burdensome to the point of overwhelm and burnout. If you do not keep your stress in check, it *will* cause many problems, including a significant decrease in your mind power.

How This Killer Affects Your Energy

Stress is a form of energy that encourages contractions. Think about it: anytime you are stressed, your muscles tense, and you shrink into yourself. You might even feel smaller because of how much the stress is weighing on you; when you contract, even physically, due to an emotional trigger, your energy contracts, too. As your energy contracts, your Kundalini contracts, and you reduce your awakened energies. You might even find yourself feeling completely disconnected, closed, or off-center due to the contraction.

Relieving yourself of stress is essential if you want to expand your energies to enjoy your awakening once more. Understand that you will often come across stress in your life, and every time it will cause contractions and minimize your energy. It is helpful to become aware of this to remain consistent in observing and recovering from these contractions. Consistency in this part of your life will help keep you open, receptive, and fluid and strengthen your resiliency and ability to bounce back from stressful experiences.

How to Spot the Killer

Finding the root causes of stress in your life is imperative if you will overthrow this energy and free up your mind power for more important things, like creating your dream life. Identifying stress in your life is most effective if you can discover the triggers that cause you to feel stressed in the first place to find ways to eliminate these triggers. The easiest way to locate your stress triggers is to locate the areas in your life where you feel a lack of mind power. In other words, where do you feel as though you cannot grow, or as though you have zero inspiration or energy to make a change to that area of your life?

Any area in your life where you feel as though you are struggling, or like there is no chance for you to grow or change that area of your life, is an area where you feel stressed. The reality is, you can grow and transform any location of your life, regardless of what struggles you are facing, though excess stress can make the idea of change seem impossible.

Some everyday stress triggers include:

- Fear of failure
- Fear of speaking in front of a crowd
- Fear of judgment
- Uncertainty or a lack of control
- Beliefs
- Your attitudes, opinions, or expectations

It is a good idea to brainstorm all of your likely stressors and rate them from 0-10, with 10 being the most stressful thing you could imagine. Once you know what your stressors are, it becomes a lot easier to witness them and take action so that stress is no longer a significant threat to your wellbeing or your mind power.

What to Do About It

After identifying your triggers, you must use this information to your advantage. Stress left unchecked presents a serious issue, so you must discover how you can use this information to manage existing stress and prevent future triggers from causing such significant stress in your life. Once you can manage stress in these areas, you open room for you to expand your mind power in them, enabling you to experience unparalleled growth that assists you with reaching your next level.

Before you can prepare yourself against your triggers being pulled in the future, you must learn to release and manage the stress you have accumulated from the triggers. Thoroughly releasing existing tension ensures that you approach your triggers from the point of peace, which means keeping your stress low is much more comfortable.

An excellent way to reduce immediate stress you are facing is through biofeedback. Biofeedback is a process that occurs when your body experiences a trigger that tells your brain something is wrong, effectively triggering a bout of stress. If you have been experiencing ongoing stress, the biofeedback you are likely encountering at the moment includes rapid breath, a quickened heart rate, tense muscles, and difficulty with eating or sleeping. You are essentially experiencing symptoms relating to the fight or flight mode, which is triggering your body to remain fixated on stress. Using biofeedback to reverse engineer your emotional state requires you to intentionally relax all of your stressful symptoms, so your brain receives the message that "it is okay." Relax your muscles, remove your tongue from the roof of your mouth, slow your breathing rate, eat something slowly, and give yourself time to bring calm into your body intentionally. Meditating is a great way to get relaxation into your body during a time of stress, as it provides you with the opportunity to bring peace to every aspect of your being without rejecting or forcing the pressure out of your body.

Once your body begins to experience relief from stress, you can start using your mindset to release more. The easiest way to rapidly shift your perspective on stress is to recognize stress as a natural symptom of difficult experiences. It is a temporary experience that you can seek relief from. After you have shifted your perspective around stress itself, you can move your viewpoint around the trigger that is causing you to feel stressed in the first place. Going your view around a trigger is best accomplished if you focus on creating acceptance around your motivation, rather than eliminating the trigger. This will earn you rapid results, whereas removing triggers often takes a significant amount of exposure before you start to feel any relief from those triggers.

When you know you will be facing one of your stress triggers, it can help you start engaging in the biofeedback process well in advance, so you are ready to face those triggers more peacefully. You may feel the first several times as though the biofeedback is not working because your body is used to reacting to those triggers with stress. As you continue using this approach, however, your body will begin to respond to these triggers in a more relaxed manner, which means you will be able to navigate them without such significant reactions.

Protecting Yourself From It

Protecting yourself against further stress may seem like an impossible feat, and in a sense, it is. You cannot prevent yourself from ever feeling pressure again, nor can you stop troubling things from happening to you; however, you can protect yourself by having a plan for how you will deal with stress in the future.

Part of protecting yourself against stress ensures you have optimal physical health, so your body is prepared to endure stressors as they arise. When your body is in optimal health, experiencing increased adrenaline or cortisol is not as bothersome because you are not already experiencing underlying stress due to poor health. As a result, you have more resilience toward additional stress in your life.

Another way to protect yourself against stress is to have a consistent stress management routine you use no matter what has triggered your tension. A great response to stress would be to take a breathing break, relax your muscles, and give yourself a few moments to experience calmness before facing the trigger, causing your stress. The more you repeat this healthy habit for stress management, the sooner you will experience relief from any form of stress you experience in your life.

CHAPTER 7
The Mindset Aspects Of Mind Power

When your mindset's physical foundation has been laid, the next step to building out your mind power lies in your mindset. The particularly impressive thing about mindset is that, regardless of how healthy your brain is, you will not have full access to your mind power if you do not have the right mindset. You can increase your mind power by accessing the right attitude, which enables you to create anything you desire, whether it be a specific result, a great day, or the fulfillment of a long-term goal.

You can take multiple steps to create a mindset that allows you to tap into the full extent of your mind power. From rapidly sorting through information to decide what is worth your attention and what is not, to look at what your mental patterns are and how you can use them to your advantage, there are many ways you can use your mindset to your advantage.

Awakening your Kundalini energy means you will inevitably experience a complete shift in your mindset. As soon as these energies awaken, you will start seeing yourself, others, the world around you, and the universe in a different light. Suddenly, things that once bothered you or negatively affected you will seem entirely irrelevant, and something that was once beyond your awareness will become imperative for you to focus on. You will find yourself naturally shifting into these more significant mindsets that improve your wellbeing and keep you growing toward your enlightenment.

Taking complete control over your mindset requires patience, consistency, and commitment. You have to be willing to continually work toward improving your mood for as long as it takes, regardless of how slow your results may be. The more you work toward improving your attitude with relentless consistency, the stronger your foundation will be, and the better your perspective will be overall.

How Mindset Controls Your Mind Power

Your mindset controls your mind power by telling you how to use your mind power. Regardless of how you use your perspective or not, your mind power exists. However, a person with a negative mindset is not acknowledging or tapping into their mind power. Instead, they ignore it or make excuses for why they are incapable of tapping into it, which results in them not taking action on the power they already have.

If you take the time to cultivate a healthy mindset, you give yourself the ability to acknowledge your power and use it to your advantage. You realize that there is no difference between you, Tony Robbins, Oprah Winfrey, massive government head figures, wildly successful CEOs, or anyone else who has achieved anything you desire. The same power they had to create the results they made exists within you, and you can use that power to achieve anything you want in life.

Just like they could transform their mindset, you also can change your mindset. With the right consistency, intention, and desire, you can manifest anything you wish in your life, and you can start it by imagining it, using the creative powers of your mind, and working toward it with consistency.

The Mindset That Unlocks Your Potential

The mindset that unlocks your potential is simple yet life-changing. It is rooted in a straightforward question, and with this question, you can achieve anything you desire in life. The problem is: "How can I do this?"

From a base state of being, when the average majority decides they want something in life, their initial reaction is to say "too bad," or "that's not possible." They always think something along the lines of why it would never happen, or how everything could go wrong to prevent them from getting their desired results. What they never think is, "How can I do this?" or "How can I make this happen?"

Immediately upon asking this question, you must start legitimately searching for the answers. Activate your creative power and look for ways that you could start turning the results you desire. Some of your responses may seem elaborate, impossible, or completely unreasonable, while others will seem like they could be possible. The ones that seem like they could be possible, and like they would likely get you the results you desire, are the ones you want to focus on. These are the ones that can get you the results you need and want and transform your life.

Awakening Your Kundalini Mindsets

As you awaken Kundalini, you will awaken your "Kundalini mindsets," or mindsets that are commonly seen in those that activate their energy field. The most significant change you will observe is a transformation in what you think about, and how. Suddenly, matters of the physical world will seem irrelevant to you. You no longer worry about things like poverty, lack, failure, or other commonly feared things, because you know that these are all trivial matters that cannot be healed through worry or fear. Things that used to bother you, like how someone else treated you, what they thought of you, or the circumstances you presently face, no longer matter because you realize they are not relevant to your wellbeing. The only thing relevant to your wellbeing is you and your beliefs, as well as the way you treat yourself.

You will likely find yourself starting to believe that you must treat others better and have compassion for others' journeys, as a way to show love to yourself. The kinder you are to others, and the less you concern yourself with them, the more at peace you will be in your life. Integrating these new, higher consciousness mindsets is essential to your awakening and enlightenment, so it is crucial to become aware of them and incorporate them into your life as they arise.

Incorporating a New Mindset Into Your Life

Incorporating a new mindset into your life is a work of art in and of itself. It would be best if you transformed the way you think about *everything*. A person that embraces a negative state of mind will think negatively about everything, and you must change that within yourself if you wish to unleash your mind power. You must stop thinking negatively about the commute to work, the food you eat, the people in your life, the music on the radio, the way someone looked at you, the weather, and everything else in your life. There is no room for you to think negatively about anything, as even a small amount of negative thinking can block your positive results.

Incorporate your positive thinking into everything, even that which seems completely irrelevant. Think positively about the people in the other cars, your coworkers, the weather, and the world around you. Even when everything seems to be going wrong, or it seems as though you have plenty to be cynical about, choose to be positive instead. Embracing positivity in all areas of your life, no matter how small, insignificant, or challenging it may seem, enables you to improve your mindset overall by incorporating a positive-oriented perspective into your everyday life. This way, when more significant circumstances arise, or you find yourself in need of your positive thinking skills, you have them to rely on because you have been building them in your everyday life.

CHAPTER 8
Having A Growth Mindset

A growth mindset is a term that defines one's ability to see opportunity over a lack of opportunity. When you have a growth mindset, you are naturally more willing to search for ways to overcome obstacles or opportunities to create something magnificent in your life. Even if you struggle with specific weaknesses or have experienced a setback in any area of your life, you believe that you can share something positive. So you routinely work toward bringing more positive into your life. Having a growth mindset is essential if you will embrace your mind power's full capacity, so it is essential that you work toward improving your growth mindset every day.

Growth Mindset Vs. Fixed Mindset

A growth mindset is the opposite of a fixed mindset. A growth mindset means you are looking for growth and change opportunities, while a fixed mindset means that you reject the idea change could happen. People with a fixed mindset believe everything is based on luck, there is no hope for them to experience anything different than their "fate," and they will never have the power to create anything better for themselves in their lives. If you have a fixed mindset, you block your capacity to receive your natural mind power because you refuse to acknowledge it and use it to your advantage.

Some suggest that if you have a fixed mindset, there is no way that you can move out of that. In other words, you either have a fixed mindset or a growth mindset, and you can't change which you have. Fortunately, you can feel confident that you have a growth mindset, as you are here reading this book and accepting the fact that there is a chance you could change the things you do not like about your life. In other words, you have hope. That, right there, is a critical indicator that you have a growth mindset.

In order to nurture your growth mindset and gain even more from it, there are many things you can do to expand that growth mentality and access an abundance of your mind power. You should do at least one of the following ten things every single day to expand your mind power and experience change in your life.

Kundalini and Growth Mindset

As you have discovered, many things that affect your physical and practical wellbeing affect your spiritual well being, too. The same remains true for the growth mindset and Kundalini. Simply put, one cannot fully tap into their Kundalini awakening if they are determined to believe that their present circumstances are the only thing they are capable of. It would help if you believed that you have some level of power over your wellbeing to enable yourself to lean in when you feel your awakening. Failing to lean in, or continually work toward awakening your energies, can lead to you sabotaging your awakening or contracting your powers.

Many times, people who believe awakening is a lie or that carry skepticism in spirituality and spiritual energies have a fixed mindset. Their fixed mindset leads them to think that no such thing is possible, so despite their efforts to awaken, they never actually awaken or activate their energy because they cannot let go. You must be willing to lean into your growth mindset and your awakening if you experience the full power of Kundalini in your life. Below are some excellent steps you can take to cultivate your growth mindset to further activate your Kundalini energy.

Be Conscious About What You Feed Your Mind

You must do every day of your life and be conscious of what you are feeding your mind. The thoughts you think to yourself, and the content you consume from the world around you are all feeding your mindset. If you are continually thinking negative things to yourself or feeding into your fears, you block your growth mindset and prevent yourself from tapping into your fullest capacity. Likewise, if you are consuming negative news, following people you dislike, or regularly talking to negative people, you are wasting your mind power on self-limiting negativity. Unfollow accounts that do not support your growth; speak to yourself in an empowering manner and avoid news or people routinely feeding you with negative information. When you are conscious about the content you consume and how you speak to yourself, you provide yourself with the range you need to grow, rather than shrink.

Work on Your Desire

Your mind is full of desires, and there are plenty of passions you could be pursuing right now. Unlike other goals, you truly desire built-in motivation because you are already eager to turn results out of those goals. Your desire, in and of itself, is motivating. The more you work toward fulfilling your desires and creating more passion in your life, the more you support yourself with achieving a positive outcome in life. Even if you do not presently have any goals associated with your desires, explore your passions, and create skills surrounding your desires. The more you sink into a passion and fill your life with it, the more you will develop goals that genuinely fuel you, and have the motivation to fulfill those goals, too.

Have the Right Sources

A lack of knowledge can prevent you from moving forward in your life because you genuinely do not know how to. No matter how much you might consider possible routes to success, if you do not know actually to put a foot on the pavement and turn results, it can block you from doing anything with that desire. Ensure that you access adequate resources to learn about the necessary tools to fulfill your desires and then use that knowledge to help move you forward. Any resource you access for learning should be one that promotes your ideas and encourages you to create your desired results; otherwise, you are not following your desires.

Embrace a Drive to Learn

If you have reached a point in your life where you have become relatively comfortable with mediocrity, it is time to change that. You need to embrace a drive to learn, and that hunger for knowledge should be as massive as you can keep it. To incorporate a lesson that Grant Cardone routinely teaches his followers, consider your current thirst for knowledge, and 10x it. In other words, blow it up to ten times the size of your present need, and aim to fulfill *that* drive, rather than the one you are presently working with. The more you can drive yourself to get excited and learn more, the greater your knowledge will be, and the stronger your results, too.

Stay Open and Flexible

Life will never go as you planned it. Fear and negative self-talk will hold you back, but they are not the only things that will hold you back. If you are unwilling to take steps forward because you are rigid in how you believe it should happen, or you are not open to the idea of change, you are blocking your mind power. Mind power occurs when you are flexible, honest, and willing to embrace change as it is needed. As you discover new knowledge or information, you will find that your understanding of how things should be done will change, too. Staying flexible ensures that you can seamlessly move into a new path and continue growing toward your desires, rather than remaining trapped in a current path that is not optimal or functional.

Be Creative and Successful

If you can imagine yourself with happiness at any point in the future, be creative enough to imagine yourself being happy now, and allow yourself to experience that success in the present. Far too many people believe that their happiness exists in the next milestone and believe that thanks to their mind power, they will be able to achieve that milestone successfully, and then they will feel good. Unfortunately, this keeps you from feeling good in the present, which keeps you from achieving your desired results. That's right: feeling good is a significant part of activating your mind power and creating your desired results. Allow yourself to feel good about who you are and where you are at right now and use that positive energy to fuel you to do even better. In the long run, this is a far more sustainable approach than always placing your happiness in the hands of the future.

Release Others' Influence Over You

Our modern world mostly relies on the influence of others. People affect us about what to like, what to buy, where to vacation, what jobs to aspire to, what interests to have, and everything else you can imagine. Being influenced is not necessarily bad, but being blindly influenced is not useful to your wellbeing. You must release others' influence over you if you have ultimate control over your own life and wellbeing. This means that you should not only tune out significant influencers such as those we see on social media and in Hollywood, but also the private influencers you have in your own life, too. Tune out the sound of family, friends, and anyone else who is attempting to influence you, especially if their influence does not lead you to create the results you desire. Focus only on yourself and what you want, and let everything else fade into the background. In other words, become your influencer.

An excellent way to gain control over yourself and eliminate others' influence over you is to engage in mindfulness. A daily mindfulness practice will allow you to check-in with yourself, identify where you have been authentic and where you have been influenced, and come back to your personal center. There, you can make choices intentionally and have a greater level of control over yourself.

The best way to implement a mindfulness practice into your daily routine is to have periodic check-ins, as well as the end of day reviews. During your periodic check-ins, you will simply be doing a quick mental check-in with yourself. Each hour, spend 1-2 minutes observing how you feel, what you are thinking about, and how you are behaving. If you recognize any area with unwanted influence, adjust how you approach that area, so you are in alignment with yourself and your genuine desire. During your end of day reviews, you want to go deeper. Bring out your journal, relax, and write down all of the significant choices you made in your day, and why. This is an excellent opportunity to reflect on what influenced you throughout the day, and whether or not you were consciously or subconsciously influenced. If you realize you were subconsciously influenced, that is a great opportunity to review how the influence occurred and bring awareness to this area of your life so you can refrain from experiencing such influence in the future. This way, you regain conscious control over yourself and your wellbeing.

Surround Yourself With Positivity

As with releasing people's influence over you, it can be useful to surround yourself with people and materials that will influence you in a positive manner. Surround yourself with people who are also interested in unlocking their mind power, increasing their growth mindset, and stepping into their fullest potential. As well, focus on consuming more materials that are positive and that encourage you to think, feel, and experience life in a way that aligns with your desires. For example, rather than scrolling social media, scroll through a book that serves your growth mindset and encourages you to create the results you desire in life. The more you surround yourself with what you want to become, the more you will influence yourself to become that person.

Speak of Present Success

One of the key tools of manifesting that warrants people's rapid results is their ability to speak in the present tense. The purpose of speaking in the present tense is not to serve some woo-woo idea that doing so magically affords you the results you desire. Rather, doing so ensures that you are focused on bringing your desires into your reality *right now*. Saying "I am getting fit" is far more ambitious and focused than saying, "I will get fit." When you say "I am getting fit," your brain becomes fixated on how you can actively get fit right now. The same goes for everything you desire. Rather than saying "I will" or "one day," say "I am" and "right now." This transition in your language is incredibly transformational and will encourage your growth mindset to kick in and start looking for ways to manifest your desires as soon as possible.

Work Through Your Resistance

Regardless of how consistently you work toward building your growth mindset, you will experience resistance. You will experience fear, doubts, negativity, and even levels of resistance that you cannot explain. At times, you might even find yourself procrastinating with no clear reason as to why you are procrastinating because that which you are avoiding doing is something you are genuinely interested in. Still, you cannot seem to get yourself in motion. Whenever you experience resistance, refrain from automatically saying, "oh well, too bad, I guess I don't want it bad enough." Instead, ask yourself, "How can I do this?" "How can I work through this resistance and create my desired results?" "How can I make this happen?"

CHAPTER 9
Deepening Your Sense Of Self

There are many theories as to what a "self" is. During periods of kundalini awakening, you are sure to feel at a loss with your sense of self. You might find yourself experiencing a disconnect from everything you have ever known, a strange sense of connection to everything around you, and confusion around your sense of identity. Enduring these experiences may be frightening, but they are all natural to the kundalini awakening and the process of expanding your mind power.

It is safe to say, however, if you are firmly grounded in your perceived self, you are likely going to feel terrified and overwhelmed by the experience of your awakening. During an awakening, there is nowhere you can run to hide from the truth. As it seeps in, you find yourself being caught off guard, forced to shift inner belief systems, and exposed to a world you likely never knew existed. It can be a lot to take in, but it can lead to a phenomenal transformation of self as you discover who you are and what potential you have in this world.

During your kundalini awakening, you will experience complete transformations in your self-orientation. First, you will experience dissolution, and then you will experience substantiation. These are both natural parts of a kundalini awakening, though they can be terrifying as you encounter them because they will completely change your life.

Dissolution of Your Self

Dissolution is the first stage of awakening, as you must willingly accept the breaking down of your present energy field if you welcome in a new plane of existence. As you engage in the dissolution process, you are likely to feel entirely unprepared and terrified about what is going on. Mental confusion, difficulty concentrating, and a tendency to slip back into old behaviors are all natural during the dissolution stage. As you embrace this new version of your identity, you find yourself experiencing sudden, intense fear about what that genuinely means. In order for one variation of yourself to be born, another must die off, which leads to a death and rebirth cycle. Naturally, you may find yourself grieving or clinging to the past, despite knowing that it is time for you to fully embrace the future.

You may find yourself leaning heavily into old coping patterns, only to realize they no longer serve you as they once did. Rather than feeling safe and stable, you feel like you are backsliding, and that creates even more tension and distress. It is essential to avoid these old habits and embrace the next stage of your life if you experience full relief from the past and the discomfort of the dissolution stage.

Those embracing the dissolution stage often feel a strange disconnect from reality, as though they are not genuinely present or there is something blocking them from the moment. You might even find yourself lacking mindfulness about your body and movements, as you begin to physically feel different in the face of change. Clumsiness, discoordination, and mistakes are all more likely to occur during this stage. You may even find yourself experiencing a certain degree of memory loss, a loss of your egoic self, and a disconnect from your sense of self-continuity.

As you embrace all of these terrifying changes, many fascinating things will also come to light. You will become absorbed with signs and symbols and their meanings, as well as the spiritual value of everything around you. With each passing symbol, you find yourself wondering what it means and how it affects your life experience. You might even find yourself intentionally asking for them and then receiving them, which indicates you are more connected than you think, even if you do not presently feel like it.

If you find yourself being overwhelmed by fits of rage, grief, and anxiety, do not fret. These are natural experiences, indicative of you releasing and purging an old sense of reality that no longer serves you or your wellbeing. From here on out, you are on a path of steady momentum, geared directly toward your awakening and the expansion of your mind power. What once was will never be again, and what has yet to come already is.

Substantiation of Your New Self

When you emerge from the dissolution stage, you find yourself embracing substantiation. This allows you to feel how change has affected your life and enjoy the most positive characteristics of an awakening. Once your old self has been purged, and the obsessions and fears associated with it have subsided, you begin to feel peace. Calmness washes over your body as you embrace a more relaxed state, and find all of your cyclical and reactive mental patterns washing away. Blocks are cleared from your mind and energy as you discover a significant sense of personal power and are able to embody it for maximum expansion of your mind power.

Those that reach this stage often find themselves engaged in a clearer and deeper perception of reality, which results in them having less emotional reactions to the world around them. Rather than being hijacked by the primal emotional brain, they are able to see things from a more logical, rational point of view. While they still have emotional experiences and intense ones at that, they are able to observe them from a different perspective and, therefore, the way they experience emotional changes.

Another impressive benefit of reaching the substantiation phase is that you are able to gain more from life itself. With the activation of this higher perception, you become more spontaneous and open to experiencing the world around you. You are no longer phased by judgment, worried about making mistakes, or held back through fear and concern around what might happen. Instead, you embody a higher level of faith and allow yourself to enjoy everything that surrounds you.

Beyond your personal experiences, your interactions with the world around you change, too. Your ability to see through a more rational and peaceful perspective means you can enjoy deeper, more significant relationships with others. When you have awakened, you no longer feel a need to cling to relationships, judge your value based on them, or avoid relationships for fear of being hurt. Instead, you feel comfortable allowing others to enjoy their life, while you also get to enjoy your life. You come together to enrich each other's lives, yet you feel equally as enriched on your own, too. This ability to feel detached from relationships makes it easier for you to genuinely enjoy them, while also showing up more authentically within them, too.

Exploring Life With Your New Identity

Receiving a new identity is empowering, especially if you take the time to explore it and invest in it. Your deepest potential for expanding mind power lies in embodying the entirety of who you are and integrating every aspect into your life. When you can observe, experience, integrate, and embrace, life becomes more enjoyable because you live a life where you genuinely accept all aspects of yourself. In this space, you no longer run away from the parts of yourself that you dislike or are afraid of. Instead, you accept them and move forward regardless, recognizing that all of these are part of what makes you the dynamic, wonderful individual that you are.

Allowing yourself to embrace this new identity begins with changing the story you have been telling yourself. Even following dissolution and substantiation, you might still be telling yourself outdated stories about who you are and what that means. Your outdated stories no longer feel right, yet they linger because you have yet to fully transform them in your mind. An excellent way to work through this and fully transition the story you are telling yourself is to sit down and journal who you think you are on a deep, core level. Do not journal about who you want to be, how you wish you perceive yourself, or how you "should" perceive yourself. Instead, write down the specific stories you have told yourself about who you are, and what that means. If you are genuinely authentic in this practice, it is likely that the things you write sound harsh and hurt. It's essential to get down these honest, painful explanations; however, as this allows you to release this story about yourself and create a new one that is more accurate.

The next stage of this practice is to adjust the story you are telling about yourself. In other words, write a new one. Again, do not write about who you want to be, how you wish to be, or who you should be. Instead, write about who you are from a positive perspective, and create an identity that feels genuinely connected with who you are. For example, if you previously identified yourself as being flaky, you might now identify yourself as being spontaneous. Or, if you previously identified yourself as being arrogant, you might now identify yourself as being confident. These shifts allow you to observe your exact personality in a new light, which means you can embrace a more optimistic, compassionate, and productive outlook on yourself.

Expanding Your Perception of Self

Your awakening brings about the most rapid, shocking changes; however, you will continue to experience an expansion in your sense of identity as you continually lean into the energies of your awakening. It is essential to avoid clinging to any aspect of your identity, even after your awakening, as doing so can prevent you from allowing further awakening to occur. Realistically, your entire life will be spent evaluating aspects of yourself and letting them fade away so new aspects can emerge. Remaining detached allows you to comfortably release pieces of yourself as they no longer fit so you can embody your new self on a continuous basis.

An excellent way to expand your mind power and embrace your ever-changing self is to regularly engage in a ritual that enables you to see your most recent version of self. Each day, week, or month, spend time writing about who you were and who you are. Keep your story fresh and relevant, and continue to update it as you work through different blocks and cycles of growth. This ensures your perception of self remains authentic and serves you in achieving further growth, as you are no longer holding yourself back with outdated stories. Beyond writing down your new story, be sure to assert it to yourself on a regular basis, so you genuinely believe it, embody it, and experience it in your everyday life.

CHAPTER 10
Using Your Mind As A Problem Solver

The average person uses their mind to process day to day activities, rarely straying away from habit and routine. While there is power in consistency, there is a lack of power when it comes to remaining consistent for a routine you did not intentionally pick, nor create. Far before modern times, man has been succumbing to pre-canned systems that determine how he will live and what he will do with his life. Authority figures have long controlled people by keeping them as a part of the majority, rather than allowing them to become authority figures, often for fear of losing control. These are all excellent resemblances of those that have yet to experience their awakening, as they hold fast to control for fear of losing their grip on others'. Of course, once you are awake, you realize there is no such thing as control, so your focus adverts away from that and toward something far more peaceful and fulfilling.

One of the most empowering journeys you can take following your awakening is the path of problem-solving. Each of our lives is filled with a series of complex issues that drive us to experience various challenges in our everyday lives. It can be easy to remain a victim of these circumstances, especially if you lack awareness around how you can reasonably shift these issues. Fortunately, every problem you face can be solved, and you have the exact power you need to solve those challenges. That power is rooted within your mind and activated through your kundalini awakening.

The Path of Ascended Problem Solving

Prior to their awakening, people often trouble themselves with solving the problems of others or perceiving others as being the root cause of their own problems. Attempting to micromanage others, and blaming others, are two tell-tale signs of a person that has yet to embrace their full awakening. When you approach life from this angle, you are attaching yourself to lower vibrational energy that can actually interrupt the extent of your mind power and sabotage your wellbeing. To fully tap into your awakening and activate your higher powers, you must be willing to embrace a different perspective when addressing problems.

Ascended problem-solving means you no longer look outside of yourself to control or blame others; instead, you look within yourself and seek to deepen your self-control. Your individual problems also shift, as you realize your original concerns were not your genuine concerns. For example, prior to your dissolution, you may have believed your issues were rooted in you being ugly, unlucky, uneducated, or unworthy. Following your awakening, you realize these are not genuine problems and that they never were to begin with. Instead, your likely problems are a lack of self-acceptance, self-appreciation, self-love, and self-motivation. These deeper issues are far more complex and damaging than the issues you previously believed you had.

Beyond seeing the truth behind your troubles, ascended problem solving also allows you to approach it from entirely new energy. Devolved problem solving typically involves you bullying and belittling yourself, and frequently criticizing yourself for things you cannot control. This self-abuse is intended to stimulate change when all it does is make you feel bad about who you are and prevent you from embracing growth. Ascended problem-solving looks like addressing your issues with love and compassion. Rather than abusing yourself for your behaviors, you can witness how your patterns are limiting you and lovingly correct them. Your focus, then, is not on solving problems but supporting your growth.

Achieving ascended problem-solving skills is a practice in itself, as it can be habitual to address your challenges from a self-abusing place. It is essential to approach your problem solving from a grounded, centered place, by focusing on how you can support yourself in having a more positive experience, rather than focusing on how you can prevent yourself from having a negative experience.

Discovering a New Way for Everything

Awakening your ascended problem-solving skills enables you to discover a new way of doing virtually everything in your life. Until now, you have likely been living your life based on other's expectations and what you believed you had to do in order to survive. It can be challenging to realize that nearly every aspect of who you are and what you do, is driven by other people and the expectations they placed on you throughout your life. Recognizing this enables you to intentionally assess each area of your life and design a lifestyle that suits your genuine needs.

Understand that every one of us has unique needs. As you discovered through kundalini and Ayurveda, your energy is unique to you and requires different tools to help you achieve significant balance within yourself. If you desire to achieve full enlightenment, you must become aware of your own energy and intentionally guide it toward a level of balance that serves your expansion. Each aspect of your life, and how you show up for your life, is infused with energy, and your intention allows you to take control over that energy and guide it in a meaningful way.

As you embody intentional energy, avoid rushing to infuse every aspect of your life with it. In doing so, you overwhelm yourself, throw yourself off course, and make it more challenging for you to embrace change. Instead, focus on essential areas of your life first, and allow yourself to expand from there. This way, you experience an intentional change in these key areas, and that change continues to flow out into every area of your life over time. Remember, enlightenment is a journey, not a race, and there is no shame in taking it at your own pace. Walk the path of growth at your own speed, and trust in the process. As long as you listen to your higher soul and trust your energy to guide you, you will find your way to expand mind power.

Becoming the Brightest Version of Yourself

Desiring to be better than everyone else is an egoic wish that naturally fades away as your kundalini energy awakens. There is no difference between yourself and others, nor is there any way to quantify who is better or worse. Finally, there is no reason to quantify such knowledge, as there is no value to being the best or the worst; these are merely ways we attempt to gauge ourselves and create a sense of false pride through our accomplishments. Rather than trying to be better than anyone else, focus on becoming the brightest version of yourself.

It is vital to use terms like "brightest" rather than "best," as describing yourself as being your best self suggests that you also have the worst self, which indicates you have yet to integrate all aspects of yourself. Further, desiring to be your best self means you see yourself as existing in your worst self, and you essentially push yourself away from becoming your best self by always believing that you have yet to get there. By desiring to be your brightest self each day, you embody this bright energy and accept all aspects of yourself as they are. In this, you solve many of your issues simply by accepting who you are and the experiences you have in life.

To become the brightest version of yourself, look for ways to live your day to day life as intentionally as possible. How can you show up authentically? What can you do to enjoy yourself more? Where can you embrace your autonomy? How can you gain more out of each moment? What can you do to support others? Where can you show up more mindfully? Living in alignment with the answers to each of these questions enables you to solve your problems from an ascended perspective and enjoy a higher quality of life. They also support you with expanding your mind power and elevating your kundalini awakening, as you are actively taking charge and embodying the benefits of the awakening itself. As you continue to integrate these benefits into your life, they continue to expand and provide you with greater value.

Expanding Your Power to Others

The devolved self always wants to be better than others, which means it wants to hoard power and avoid sharing anything with anyone else. This is evident in many self-serving authoritative figures; however, it can also be seen in many people existing as a part of the average majority. As you embrace your awakening, you realize that there is no distinction between yourself and others; we are all one. What makes you a human and the experiences you have are the same as what makes me a human, and the experiences I have. While we may have our own personalities, memories, life paths, individual experiences, goals, dreams, relationships, perspectives, and otherwise, at our core essence, we are the same. It is likely that, had I been born into your exact experience, I would have been exactly the same as you are, and you would have also been exactly the same as I am had you been born into mine. At our roots, we are all humans embodying the human experience in one way or another.

Because we are all the same, the way we treat each other heavily affects the way we treat ourselves, too, and vice versa. The way you treat yourself will influence the way you treat others. If you want to become an excellent problem solver and ascend through all of your troubles, it pays to discover how you can assist yourself while also assisting others. Becoming of service to others enables you to better understand their perspectives, educate them on a better way of living, and support them with experiencing more from life.

The key to expanding your power to others is to remain detached from the experience. In other words, serve others when it reflects as a sign of you loving yourself, and never otherwise. When you serve someone else because you genuinely gain joy out of it or because you desire to see the benefit touch their lives, you feel good about helping them. Then, you never feel as though you are being taken advantage of or treated as an unpaid servant. Instead, you feel as though you have shown up for yourself and another at the same time, and you both gain benefit from that.

Remaining detached also means that you do not feel as though you have to micromanage another or force them to receive your support. If someone declines your assistance, you can lovingly accept this and move on. From there on out, you remain detached, so you can allow them to fulfill their own life experience and learn in their own way or not. Because you have granted them the freedom to experience life as they need to, you also grant them the gift of unconditional love and acceptance, which are incredibly valuable to each of us. Plus, when you can unconditionally love and accept another, you can also unconditionally love and accept yourself.

CHAPTER 11
Your Ego Needs Checking

According to the kundalini tradition, the ego must die if you will fulfill your path of enlightenment. The ego is considered the anchor of the unevolved human self, which often serves as a root cause for most suffering. It has been reported that your ego will frequently "flare-up" in an effort to regain control, effectively preventing you from shedding it and living in alignment with truth, rather than ego. The trouble is, your ego has been programmed by society for years and is designed to prevent you from fully stepping into greatness. In most cases, your ego will effectively hold you back and keep you playing small, using emotions such as pride and duty to prevent you from necessary growth and awakening.

As you embody your kundalini awakening, there becomes an inevitable point where your ego must die or, at the very least, be demoted, so it no longer controls you. When you effectively shed your programmed ego, you gain the opportunity to listen carefully to your higher energies and follow the truth, rather than your programming. This concept may seem far-fetched, particularly if you only recently began your awakening experience; however, it is necessary to understand. So long as you continue to allow your ego to run the show, you will succumb to the ego's limitations.

Checking your ego means discovering how to let it naturally fade, to the point of eventual death. The process does not have to be fast, though it can be. It does not have to be painful, though it usually will be. Because you currently lack the ascension that comes from having released your ego, you find yourself struggling to surrender to the process wholly. The ability to surrender as deeply as you need to is often learned and achieved by the time the ego has been fully released. Until then, it is best to embrace the process and trust in the flow, even if the flow sometimes feels painful, challenging, or impossible.

Shedding the Programmed Ego

There are two versions of ego: the programmed ego and the primal ego. The primal ego is something we are all born with, and it is designed to help distinguish the difference between yourself and others. Allowing you to see your individuality means your ego roots you in the present reality, showing you that the human condition includes several individuals taking their own journey to the same place, more or less. This perspective is necessary, as it enables you to see and participate in the same reality everyone else is participating in, which helps connect you to the rest of society.

Over time, your ego is programmed by society. As it continues to shape and identify present reality, your ego evolves to gain a more dynamic understanding of what that actually means. Rather than merely seeing yourself as being separate from everyone else, you now start to formulate stories around what that means and how you can minimize your separateness by adapting to the common values of society. In many cases, these values are not the genuine values of each individual, rather the common values of the unawakened many.

Shedding the programmed ego is the first step of ego death, as it enables you to release pride from aspects of yourself that are not relevant to your well being or your higher life experience. As this aspect of your ego is deprogrammed and released, you gain the ability to see life through a purer set of eyes. In many cases, it feels as though you see the world with childlike wonder because you have released the pain and pressures associated with societal expectations and commands.

The process of shedding your programmed ego will naturally begin when you commence your kundalini awakening. As you continue to awaken, your programmed ego will continue to be shed. In some cases, the shedding will happen as a natural evolution that requires minimal effort on your behalf. Aside from embracing the awakening and embodying the changes, no further effort is required for you to experience the shedding of your programmed ego.

In some cases, however, the shedding process feels more complex than that. When shedding the ego feels more challenging, the best thing you can do is be gentle with yourself and love yourself through the process. Rather than attempting to control, judge, or limit the grief, pain, or distress you are feeling, accept it, and recognize it as being a part of the process. Allow yourself to compassionately and productively feel through and express those emotions, then release them. Once they are gone, you will feel a renewed sense of peace and relief in that part of your existence.

Preventing Your Ego From Holding You Back

As you embrace the ego death process, there will be a deep inner voice demanding you to "go back." This voice will command you to return to safety, avoid your growth, and stop looking crazy. Essentially, it will say everything it feels it needs to in order to prevent you from bravely walking forward and embodying your awakening. This voice *is* your ego, and the many things it is saying reflect your egos desire to remain intact. As far as it is concerned, it is a staple to your wellbeing as it protects you from doing anything wrong and keeps you connected to a greater society. This is precisely the problem, however, as it is keeping you connected in a low vibrational way. You can connect in a higher way if you release the ego itself.

During the death process, you can prevent the ego from holding you back by slipping as deep into surrender as possible. Through surrender, you find trust, and in the trust, you discover the strength; you need to allow the process to take its course so you can be relieved from the pain of your ego. Anytime you find yourself enduring a particularly painful, self-sabotaging, or mentally draining day associated with your ego death, intentionally set aside time to process your feelings. If you can, sit down with your journal and write about what you are feeling and experiencing, and recall what you are looking forward to. As you create this shift within your mind, the emotional aspect of your ego death feels less painful and more endurable. Through it, peace and shift are created.

It is especially important to become aware of your ego, holding you back anytime you actively witness this happening. Part of having a programmed ego is having one that is so sneaky that it behaves subconsciously, without you being aware of what is going on. You can rapidly bring this into your awareness using two techniques: choosing to place your awareness on the behavior of your ego, and observing your life for points of resistance, lack, or struggle. If you experience any of these three things, you can be confident that your ego is running the show in that area of your life.

Drawing your awareness into these behaviors that are typically rooted in your subconscious means you can consciously ascend these behaviors, allowing your ego to die off even more. Once they have been brought into your awareness, complete your journaling process for uncovering them, understanding them, and redirecting yourself toward new, more efficient behaviors. The more consistent you are, the better.

Creating an Egoless Future

The goal of kundalini is to reach a point in your life where you no longer have an ego. The ego death is an ultimate symbolism of enlightenment, as it indicates that you have fully released the lower vibrational elements of being a human. You are now pure enough to enter the kingdom of heaven, so says tradition. Despite the tremendous value of ego death, it is essential to understand that this process does not happen rapidly, nor would you want it to. While it can, and it can even be painless if you manage to fully succumb, most people will not react well to rapid or sudden ego death. Instead, such a rapid death could lead to them experiencing insanity, delusions, or other conditions suffered by those who have had their understanding of reality suddenly torn away from them. To say it is traumatizing would be an understatement.

Continually focusing on your ego death and working toward facilitating it means that, eventually, your entire ego will have died off. Following your natural pace and remaining consistent in your actions means you can look forward to eventually experiencing a total ego death. This may happen in your present lifetime, or it may happen many lifetimes from now when you have had an adequate opportunity to work through all of your karma and release yourself from it.

It is reasonable to understand that not everyone will experience total ego death, nor does everyone want to. For many, their attachment to the human condition keeps them from wanting to experience full ego death, and that is okay. Through kundalini, you can still expand your mind power by shedding the programmed ego in favor of a deprogrammed or primal ego. The unity of a primal ego with a self-aware mind leads to an impressive state of mental expansion, which allows you to tap into the fullness of your personal power.

CHAPTER 12
Happiness Is Your Choice, Make It

Studies have shown that happiness plays an incredible role in your mental health, yet the way you approach happiness may not be serving you. Knowing how to create your own happiness, and live with a lack of happiness, enables you to gain the true value of this beautiful emotion. Further, it allows you to apply an expansive perspective to it and embody the lessons that happiness has to teach you.

Regardless of what anyone says, happiness is a choice that you get to make. Happiness is not linked to your income, appearance, material possessions, perceived personal value, worthiness, or anything else. Happiness is solely linked to your decision to be happy, no matter what.

The Real Path to Happiness

The real path to experiencing genuine happiness is to stop pursuing happiness. As with anything, the more you try to pursue it, the more you reinforce the lack of it in your subconscious mind. Because you are always seeking happiness, your mind concludes that you must presently be without happiness. After all, you would not seek it if you already had it.

Through the lessons of kundalini, you have discovered so much about embodying the energy and embracing all that this energy has to offer you. Applying these same lessons to happiness enables you to tap deeply into the power of your mind and make meaningful choices to your wellbeing. It starts with realizing that happiness is not something you get to; it is something you choose to make and hold within yourself in each individual moment.

Start right now. As you sit here, reading this book, close your eyes and take a few deep breaths into your diaphragm. Then, once you experience the presence of peace in your mind, choose to feel happy in this moment. Continue focusing on the choice of being happy right now until you genuinely feel happy within yourself. Hold onto this decision and continue about your daily life. The real secret to feeling happy is deciding to be happy right now, regardless of what is going on in your life.

How Happiness Improves Your Health

Happiness is not only a spiritual experience; it is also one that improves your wellbeing in a tangible manner. Studies have shown that when you are happy, you are more resilient, have a better immune system, and experience less pain than the average person. Happiness also improves your mental health, supporting you with offsetting depression, anxiety, and other mental health conditions. It can also boost your memory, creativity, and mental clarity.

To create more happiness in your life as a way to boost your health, all you need to do is focus on the things that make you happy right now. Previously, you may have believed that your happiness would be determined by external circumstances beyond your control, or beyond the present moment. Now, you must realize that your happiness can be created right now by things that cost you nothing. Remember a pleasant memory, smell something you like, eat tasty food, have a positive conversation with a friend, say something nice to yourself, or find a reason to laugh in the moment. These are all excellent ways to make yourself happy in the moment, so you can experience the benefits of success right away, regardless of what is going on in your life.

Consciously Choosing to Be Happy

As with anything, consciously choosing to be happy in each moment requires practice. It takes a significant amount of energy to increase your conscious awareness, let alone with the intention of monitoring and adjusting your day to day life. If you wish to consciously choose to be happy, you must not only expand your conscious awareness but discover how to use it to adjust your behavior.

To expand your conscious awareness, you must simply become knowledgeable in controlling your awareness filter. This filter is attuned to recognize anything you ask it to, and it is incredibly efficient with its job. Think about it, before you bought the current car you drive, it is likely that this specific model of car did not stand out to you on the road. Once you started thinking about buying it, and after you acquired it, you started seeing it everywhere. Why? Because it has been brought into your conscious awareness as a substantial piece of information. This is a prime example of your awareness filter.

Expanding your consciousness starts with adjusting your awareness filter to look for areas of opportunity. Do this by recognizing your symptoms of happiness and setting your awareness filter to look for signs of happiness. Then, go through your normal daily experience and observe how your awareness filter automatically draws your attention to your symptoms of happiness. This is an excellent sign, as it means you are fully capable of becoming aware of anything you desire, based on what you request from your filter.

Now that you can comfortably observe periods of happiness, see if you can adjust your filter to become aware of times when you are not happy. Perhaps there are specific points in your day when you can benefit from happiness, yet you are not yet making the decision to feel that way. Recognize the symptoms that indicate that you have arrived at that point, then draw your awareness filter to this part of yourself. Anytime you observe these choice points in action, use your breath (Prana) and the power of choice to embody happiness, even if happiness seems like the most challenging decision to make in that moment.

Continue making the conscious decision to bring happiness into your life. As often as you can, observe areas where you would benefit from greater happiness and make a choice to create happiness in that space. If you cannot invoke happiness through a simple breath, consider ways you can adjust those areas of your life to set yourself up for happiness in advance. This way, you intentionally create a more positive experience, rather than allowing yourself to continually fall victim to unhelpful patterns.

Embracing a Lack of Happiness

Happiness is not a lifelong emotion. No emotions are. Each emotion you feel is fleeting and ends sooner than you likely think it will. Increasing your awareness around this ensures that, as you experience emotions, you also experience detachment from them. This way, you allow them to live out their natural course and provide yourself with an abundance of space to feel and experience life in its entirety.

Acknowledging that happiness is among one of the many temporary emotions you experience means you accept that there will be periods in your life that lack happiness altogether. When you are grieving, experiencing pain, or suffering for any reason, for example, you may feel an absence of happiness in your life. This does not imply that you cannot look for reasons to be optimistic, but it does mean that you are unlikely to experience genuine happiness in that moment. At times, you may be comfortable in that lack of happiness and unwilling to do anything to change it, which is acceptable, healthy, and normal.

When you experience a lack of happiness in your life, it is essential that you do not make any judgments around this. Avoid judging your emotions, your preferences, or the way you navigate that life experience. Instead, embrace it, accept it, and consider your chosen approach as being the one you need to embody the experience of "being okay." Being okay is achievable in any state, so long as we are open to accepting the emotions we are feeling.

Should you ever feel troubled by your lack of happiness, recall that happiness always comes back, just as sadness always ends. The sooner you surrender to your emotions, the sooner you can express them and heal through them as you return to a more positive, pleasant state. It is perfectly reasonable to understand that experiencing a lack of happiness means that the return of your happiness is far more gratifying, as it provides you with a renewed appreciation for the feeling itself. Be patient, compassionate, and loving toward yourself, and all will pass, soon.

CHAPTER 13
How You Treat Them Is How You Treat You

A beautiful concept that the average human frequently fails to recognize is that the way you treat others equates to the way you treat yourself, and vice versa. Generally speaking, if you have a positive, wholesome relationship with yourself, you will have an easier ability to have a positive and wholesome relationship with others, too. If you wish to experience more love, compassion, empathy, reliability, permanency, or anything else in your relationships with other people, you must embrace that in your relationship with yourself. Further, if you wish to see and experience the best in humanity, you must see and experience the best within yourself. Expanding the quality of your relationship with yourself directly expands the quality of your relationship with others, allowing you to gain greater fulfillment from life.

Why Your Intrapersonal Relationship Matters

They say that in order for someone else to love you, you must first love yourself. This is an ineffective way of getting the point across, as the more accurate message is that the more you love yourself, the more you can observe and receive love from others'. How much you love yourself holds zero impact on others' capacity to love you, but one hundred percent impact on your capacity to accept that love from others'.

We all desire high-quality relationships filled with mutual love, respect, compassion, acceptance, understanding, and growth. To embody that with someone else provides us with the opportunity to experience the highest potential in our relationships, which we believe will make us feel better. Once again, there is a delusional belief here. Those who have yet to awaken will likely believe that the improved feelings come from the higher-quality relationships with others when it actually comes from the quality of the relationship we have with ourselves in order to facilitate those improved relationships.

Simply put, you cannot engage in these high-quality relationships if you are not first in a place with yourself where you can reasonably show up to these relationships in a healthy manner. If you bring in limiting patterns or behaviors, you are introducing sabotage to your relationships and limiting the extent to which you can receive from them. You must learn to fully detach from your relationships to gain the most out of them, and to achieve this detachment; you must have a strong enough relationship within yourself to feel safe doing so. If you lack that strong connection to yourself, releasing your connection from others' feels impossible because these relationships are fulfilling needs, you believe you cannot fulfill yourself. The trouble is, your inability to fulfill them yourself means you settle for anyone willing to try, and you are always landing in unhealthy relationships with unhelpful expectations since you are asking people for something they genuinely cannot offer.

Becoming your own rock means you can independently fulfill your needs, which makes your relationships more supplemental than anything. Yes, they maintain a necessary value in your life; however, you no longer need to attach to them to suck as much energy out of them as possible. Instead, you can allow people to be themselves and enjoy their own life experiences without having to demand their time, attention, or change, because you, too, can enjoy your own life experience in your own way. This autonomy and respect create space for high quality, healthy relationships to exist between yourself and others.

Expanding the Quality of Your Relationship to Self

Fixating on how to improve your relationships with others is the wrong approach to take when it comes to creating a positive link between how you treat yourself and others. So long as you continue to focus on external relationships as a way to facilitate these improvements, you will continue to experience limitations as you wait on other people to behave the way you need them to for you to change. Practically speaking, this is an ineffective approach to improving your relationships.

A more appropriate and effective approach is to improve your relationship with yourself, which will naturally improve your relationship with others. Further, it will welcome more people into your life that are a better fit for you, which will make enjoying enriching and meaningful relationships more accessible. How you improve your relationship with yourself entirely depends on what your present relationship looks like. Though there are plenty of excellent steps you can take to get started.

One excellent way to develop a positive relationship with yourself is to express gratitude for yourself and your body, especially. Being grateful for the body you have and the experiences you create is a wonderful way to develop a closer connection with yourself. You should also be kind to yourself, including your mind, emotions, body, and spirituality. Say empowering things to yourself, take care of yourself, and engage in practical measures to support your wellbeing from a physical vantage point. In kundalini, physical activities are fundamental because people have long known that your body matters to your wellbeing. If you desire to achieve greater enlightenment, you must have the healthiest body you can to get there. The purer your body, the purer your energy and the more aligned your field will be.

It also pays to release your inner perfectionist and judgment. Attempting to be perfect at everything effectively keeps you from pursuing anything, for fear of enduring the messy beginner stages or the mistakes that come with increasing your skill in any area of your life. Your judgment feeds your perfectionism but also serves to sabotage you in many other ways, as well. For example, your judgment increases separation between yourself and others, damages your relationship with people you care about, harms your relationship to yourself, and positions you as a bully in many people's stories. Judgment does nothing to aid your wellbeing, only to hinder it. If you want to improve your relationship with yourself, you must cut judgment out completely.

Lastly, you need to notice and redirect your inner critic. Your inner voice is often powered by your ego and serves to protect you by invoking fear and other limiting emotions that prevent you from faithfully pursuing your destined path. As you shed your programmed ego and work toward developing a positive relationship with yourself, you must become observant of your inner voice and correct it whenever you need to. Always redirect it toward more loving, fulfilling, and nurturing voices, so it supports you. The more empowering you are toward yourself, the stronger your relationship with yourself will be.

Unconditional Love and Acceptance of Others

Expanding your relationship with yourself will inevitably expand your love and acceptance of others. As you witness the complexities of self-love and come to understand the impact of your experience, you will discover it is far easier for you to accept others that are also struggling with this path. Your heightened awareness from your awakening also provides you with the opportunity to lovingly accept anyone that has not yet chosen or is actively resisting the path of awakening themselves to their full energy. In fact, this is essential as it not only increases the quality of your relationships but also dramatically expands your mind power.

As you release your need to worry about others and how they are behaving or the way they are affecting you, you increase your expendable mental space. Now that you no longer have to monitor and manage everyone else, you can focus on deepening your self-awareness and monitoring and managing yourself. Here, you can use this level of awareness to expand your relationship to yourself, while also allowing that to expand the quality of your relationship to others.

A wonderful way to begin expressing unconditional love and acceptance toward others also happens to be an excellent tool for times when expressing these unconditional emotions seems challenging or even impossible. At times, particularly when you are upset by the way someone else is behaving, it is necessary to take additional action toward releasing feelings of resistance and opening up to feelings of unconditional love and acceptance.

The tool best used is called loving kindness meditation. This meditation is used to express love and acceptance to people, especially those we are troubled by, so we can dissolve our resistance and increase our own good vibes. Kundalini especially embraces this, encouraging you to release others' from your mind so you can address your own karma while they address theirs.

To engage in a loving kindness meditation, start by relaxing and engaging in meditative breath. When you have reached a point where you feel calm and centered, you can begin expressing loving kindness to anyone and anything that crosses your mind. Continue expressing it until you genuinely feel a sense of love and kindness toward that person or thing. An excellent way to invoke this is to simply repeat, "I love you and accept you unconditionally," which draws your focus and encourages you to embody these feelings. You may have to do multiple sessions for particularly stubborn experiences; however, you will begin to embody significantly higher levels of love and acceptance toward others through this repeated practice.

Empowering All From Your Expanded Awareness

Ascending into a higher relationship with yourself and others means exploring how you can lovingly empower yourself and others from this new state of awareness. One significantly meaningful way of empowering others, and yourself, is to hold space for everyone to be who they genuinely are. People each have their own unique qualities, strengths, attractive features, weaknesses, and ugliness. No one is exempt from experiencing both the positive and negative aspects of being a human, not even yourself. Rather than holding unreasonable expectations that everyone abandons their weaknesses and ugly sides in favor of their strengths and attractive sides, it is more meaningful to hold space for people to simply be. This way, you and all who surround you do not feel pressured to hide their ugliness and flaws from the world around them.

In holding space for others, be willing to forgive their mistakes and continue to love and accept them unconditionally, even if they have messed up. Hold that same level of forgiveness for yourself, too. Believe in everyone's ability to be a better person, and do what you can to uplift people so they can witness that in themselves, too. Do not punish yourself, or them, if it fails. Instead, lovingly accept where they are at, and that you are incapable of forcing anyone to do anything, at any time. Whenever you see someone genuinely exert effort into something, praise them and celebrate their wins. Even if their wins are small, or they themselves cannot see the value of those wins, celebrate them. Celebrate yourself abundantly, too.

As you continue to uplift and empower others through your unconditional desire to support, love, and accept, you will witness the quality of your relationships to yourself and others growing. Through this, you experience greater mind power and an expanded ability to enjoy all that life has to offer.

CHAPTER 14
Becoming Your Biggest Cheerleader

Kundalini *is* a journey to self-empowerment. Yes, it enables you to improve the quality of your relationships with others and the experiences you have with the world around you, but the number one purpose is to improve everything for yourself. By embodying this level of selfishness, you provide yourself with the ability to become your own biggest cheerleader. Through that, you naturally show up in a more meaningful way for the world around you, too.

Feeling the Entirety of Your Presence

Awakening your kundalini means you are exposed to the dynamic energies that make up every aspect of who you are, from your body to your soul, and even your connection to god. Your ability to cheer yourself on is amplified when you realize your presence is far greater than a mere body with a persistent voice living in its head. Grasping the entirety of who you are means recognizing that there is so much more of you to cheer on, and so much more of you cheering when you do. It is no longer just you and your history of life experiences and external influences. Now, it is you, your higher self, your god-self, and the presence of your god themselves. Your team is vast and entirely rooted within yourself.

Upon awakening and activating these energies, you realize that life is much bigger than you may have previously realized. The vastness of life itself means that everything is worth celebrating, including you. Further, you realize you are deeply supported in being yourself and celebrating the experience of showing up as this brilliant individual. Rather than looking to others for validation, love, and acceptance, you can comfortably look toward yourself and confidently receive all of these and more.

As you engage in your daily meditation sessions, welcome in the entirety of your presence both earthly and beyond. Use your breath to invoke life force energy and feel the connection between yourself and the divine, and allow that connection to empower you. Through this, you will find many reasons to celebrate.

Celebrating Yourself on Every Level

The unawakened individual celebrates only the tangible wins they experience, particularly those that can earn them status. For example, they happily celebrate career promotions, engagements, new homes, children, and other such status symbols. However, they rarely celebrate the seemingly lesser things that carry just as much, if not more of an impact on their overall growth. For example, they fail to celebrate their smaller actions taken toward achieving their goals, such as the daily tasks they complete to get them closer to their win.

Learning to celebrate everything about yourself, right down to the smallest details of your physical, mental, emotional, and spiritual growth is invaluable to your success. As you celebrate yourself, you actively become your own biggest cheerleader. In that, you uncover an abundance of joys in life, each of which enriches your experience. For example, you find happiness, fulfillment, self-trust, self-confidence, a positive relationship with yourself, and a desire to continue doing more as you move into greater levels of expansion.

Embracing Fearlessness In Your Life

Fear is a natural, functional element of life. You experience fear because your body is wired to. Under necessary circumstances, fear provides you with the adrenaline rush required to fight or flight, allowing you to save your life from a wild tiger or a hungry bear. In modern circumstances, there are few situations where you need fear to come into play. However, you must discover how to relieve yourself of fear because it will inevitably make its way into your life anyway.

One of the fastest ways to embrace fearlessness in your life is to recognize that you have a significant energy source behind you. As you breathe in, you invoke life force energy in your very body. This unites you to your entire self, as well as the gods above. Through this, you have all the power you need to persevere through any challenge you face, no matter how significant.

Calling on this greater power to support you through life does not invoke total fearlessness, but it will drastically downplay the fear you experience while expanding your faith. This combination empowers you to move through any obstacle, as you feel as though you have a genuine reason to celebrate and cheer yourself on.

Living as Your Authentic Self

Lastly, you need to live as your authentic self. The value of a cheerleader is that they cheer you on to becoming your best, and becoming your best means living as your most authentic self. Despite you having the same essence as everyone else on earth, you are made up in a unique manner and express in a way that is different from anyone else. The offering you have for earth and other humans is also unique to you, and can only be achieved when you clear out your limitations and live in alignment with your authentic self.

As your inner cheerleader cheers you on and encourages you to embrace higher levels of being, you must oblige and embody those very energies. The more you do, the more you reinforce that you are capable and worthy of embracing these higher aspects of yourself. You also reinforce your cheerleader by following through and validating his or her power and presence in your life. Moreover, when you live as your authentic self, your inner cheerleader has more reasons to shout, "YES!"

Each of us needs a healthy dose of convincing from time to time, especially if we genuinely believe that the activity we are about to make could harm us in some way, even if only through a minor inconvenience. Embracing your inner cheerleader, playing deeply into the role, and following through on the actions your cheerleader motivates you to take are all essential ways to become the brightest version of yourself through meaningful acts of self-motivation.

CHAPTER 15
Love Conquers All... Really

At the core of expanding your mind power lies one phenomenal energy that you must embody if you wish to achieve anything. That is, love.

Love provides you with the necessary energy to move through anything, no matter how challenging or overwhelming it may be. Through love, you can ascend judgment, hate, pain, and virtually every other circumstance you are faced with. Where love exists, no negative feelings can, because there is a deep core desire to experience connection, fulfillment, and positivity in spite of anything else you might face.

In kundalini, unconditional love is said to be the way to ascension and a powerful way to overcome the limitations of the ego. Through the presence of love, you gain the capacity to move beyond attachments that keep you rooted in pain and welcome the energy of growth and positivity instead. If you wish to experience the greatness of life, you must first move into the light of love. There, you find the freedom to ascend at your own pace and in your own way.

Love to Overcome Ego

Love is a potent antidote to ego. As you continue on your journey of overcoming the programmed ego and embracing the primal ego, or ego death, you can embody love as a powerful tool. Through love, you accept all aspects of self, including that which you like and that which you do not. You dissolve all attachments to aspects of yourself that you like or dislike most, meaning you are free to move between identities and embrace an ever-expanding version of yourself.

Instead of becoming attached to the process of your ego deprogramming or death, discover how you can love yourself and your ego. Unconditionally love the value it brought you in the past, and love yourself for any challenges you faced as a direct result of your ego. Come to understand that your ego is not bad nor evil. It is merely an experience you have had that you are now willing to release in favor of feeling your best and enjoying the unconditional growth that comes with letting it go.

Unconditional Love Is the Goal

Unconditional love is, by far, the biggest goal of kundalini. This is the energy gifted to us by the heavens, and the energy we will return to when we ascend from our life experiences. Learning to embrace it in your everyday life allows you to dissolve the attachment, ascend your awareness, and live the truth in a more grounded, practical manner.

This energy also allows you to embrace the true power of your mind by erasing limiting attachments, expanding your heart toward growth, and giving you the faith and confidence you need to try new things. As you continue to expand into these new experiences and adventures, you discover more, your understanding of life deepens, and you tap into greater levels of power held within your mind.

The process of tapping into unconditional love requires you to call on the forces of your mind by sitting back and observing the many values you gain from everything in your life, even the more troubling experiences that you tend not to enjoy as much. As you begin to uncover the value of everything, whether you enjoy it or not, you realize that your life is made for you, and there is always a purpose behind everything you experience. Thus, it becomes easier to embrace everything through unconditional love, and use that love to tap into the abundance of lessons that life has to offer you.

The Eightfold Theory of Love

In kundalini, there is an eightfold theory of love, which introduces why unconditional love is so valuable in the first place. By studying the theory of love and why we require it in our lives, you expand your awareness around this empowering energy and uncover ways to embrace it in your everyday life.

The first aspect of the theory of love is the theory itself. The theory of love and hate is a simple one, outlining that we all desire to love and experience love, yet we go through phases where we are unable to maintain the flow of love, which leads to a variety of emotions, often ending in hate. From hate, we experience vengeance, and through vengeance, we reach destruction, which is where we begin to cause unnecessary chaos in our lives and the lives of others. Everything starts with love, as love is the basic law of life.

The second aspect of the theory of love is called hook and hooker, which is a game involving two or more individuals. This game is often played as a way of establishing security, which is only an illusion. In this case, one person desires to attract the love of others, and the others desire to love that individual. Through this, there seems to be a balance in love, yet there is not one. Unless all can love each other unconditionally, it is a game that no one will win.

The third aspect of the theory of love is that emotional love is not the same as unconditional love. With emotional love, you feel fulfillment in others' and reject your personal reality, making it inferior to others. In this case, you may behave like a caregiver or to value everyone else's happiness above your own, effectively sabotaging your experience with love.

The fourth aspect of the theory of love is commotional love. This is a love that interlocks with emotional fantasy and uses the ego to create habits of insecurity and attitudes with bad manners. When you engage in commotional love, you experience hollowness, shallowness, a lack of fulfillment, inferiority, anger, fear, trauma, impotency, and sleepless nights. Rather than embracing true unconditional love, you have attached yourself to a chaotic form of love that is not beneficial to anyone.

The fifth aspect of the theory of love is circumstantial love. This form of love is produced by the pressure of time and space and has the capacity to change with time and space, too. When you embody circumstantial love, you fail to embrace unconditional love because you are conditioned by the circumstances themselves.

The sixth aspect of the theory of love is real love. Real love enables you to promote, serve, and invest in another's excellence while still embodying and embracing your own excellence. Through this experience of love, you feel another's soul and understand them in a way that is deeper than you can achieve with any other form of love.

The seventh aspect of the theory of love is self-love, which accounts for an understanding of your own existence and the love you have for yourself. At the root of all that you achieve in life is self-love, which drives you to experience the freedom to engage in selflessness and unconditional love with others. This type of love is deeply fulfilling and expansive and paves the way for an entirely new experience in love.

The eighth aspect of the theory of love is infinite love, which is the love you experience when you tap into the energy of your infinite wisdom and reality. This love is often achieved once you have awakened and balanced your crown chakra, which is responsible for your connection to the divine. A wholesome connection here leads to an empowering ability to expand the infinite aspects of your love for others.

CHAPTER 16
Set Goals And Accomplish Them, Often

Setting goals is a tremendous way to motivate yourself to experience more in life and creates a brilliant opportunity to expand the power of your mind. The human mind craves to be challenged, and providing it with goals complete with obstacles is an excellent way to challenge yourself to achieve more. Through the introduction of kundalini, your approach for creating and achieving goals will transform as you embrace a new way of ascending through the many challenges of life. You still must set goals and aspire to achieve them; however, the specific goals you set and the way they have achieved changes entirely. From your heightened awareness and perspective, you realize that there are greater ways to achieve success and to pursue success that is more meaningful to you overall.

The Achieve and Integrate Cycle

Those that have yet to awaken frequently approach their goals with a steadfast desire to push through no matter what and force their way to the end. Often, they reach the end of their goals, feeling a momentary sense of happiness, followed by a deep need to pursue something else. Over time, their achievements stack, yet their sense of victory fails to stack, so they often reach a point of success accompanied by a feeling of hollowness or emptiness.

As you approach your goals from an ascended position, you embrace a cycle of growth that is associated with achieving and integrating. Essentially, this means you work toward fulfilling your goals in life while frequently pausing to allow yourself to integrate each new phase of achieving your goals. Further, you do not push toward fulfilling your goals; you attract the necessary steps to fulfill them and enable yourself to remain focused by receiving intuitive guidance and following the path of least resistance. You must still address challenges, face hardships, and overcome obstacles; however, you experience a more significant level of faith in yourself and your destiny, which allows you to follow the path confidently. Through this, you truly embrace the path of least resistance, allowing you to achieve greater heights of success in virtually every area of your life.

Setting Goals for Your Ascended Self

Setting goals for your ascended self is unlike setting goals for your pre-awakened self. Prior to your awakening, you likely fixated on goals that were associated with your status, appearance, and material gains. You might have desired a slimmer body, larger muscles, a bigger or newer house, a fancier car, a better wardrobe, or any other number of things that would have made you appear better in the eyes of others. While desiring for these things is not inherently bad, it often takes away from your ability to recognize what you truly desire.

Setting goals for your ascended self should be less focused on the external world and your status and power over others, or their opinion of you, and more focused on yourself and what you want to experience in life. This may involve the external world; however, it should be largely focused on your internal self and experiences. Goals relating to how you can experience more from life, gain more joy from each moment and deepen your mindfulness are far more impressive and impactful than goals surrounding your status or worldly achievements. Further, they bring greater levels of fulfillment and significant satisfaction when you do achieve them.

The most effective way to set these ascended goals is to ask yourself: "How do I genuinely want to feel?" Then write the answer down. Your answer to this question defines what your ascended goals should be.

Reaching the Goals Energetically

Reaching goals energetically is as important as reaching them practically. Practical goal-reaching enables you to tick that goal off your list, but if you have not embodied that goal on a deep level, it seems as though you have accomplished nothing. Rather than feeling accomplished and fulfilled, you are left feeling as though your accomplishment was not a big deal, or was not as meaningful as you hoped it would be. Through energetic investment, your goals become more meaningful, and you are able to fully embody the joy of having reached them.

Investing energetically in your goals also enables you to reach them faster. When you experience full-bodied investment in the things that matter to you, you make power moves. Rather than sitting by passively waiting for things to turn in your favor, you invest fully into making them happen. This is the energy people get into when they rapidly shift their lives and manifest their deepest desires. Through this energy, you can have a significant impact on your wellbeing. It is well worth it for you to embrace this level of energy if you want to have a massive impact on your life, and tap into the entirety of your mind power.

Embodying Your Accomplishments

Lastly, you must embody your accomplishments. There is no sense in pursuing a meaningful goal, only to let it slip and fall back to negative patterns after you have reached it. Since your goals are no longer associated with your material gains, it is more essential than ever that you invest in seeing those goals through and embodying them full-time. Creating meaningful habits around your goals is an excellent way to turn them into embodied changes, which allows you to gain the most from them.

The other benefit of embodying your accomplishments is the value it gives your mind. Practically speaking, each time you reach a goal and celebrate that win, your brain experiences a rush of dopamine that is released to reward you for your success. This dopamine rush provides you with the encouragement you need to continually pursue more of your goals, and achieve more significant accomplishments.

A powerful way to fully embody your accomplishments is to affirm your success to yourself and genuinely celebrate yourself for the win. Consider yourself as successful as you would an Olympian that just won their first gold medal, and celebrate yourself with as much gusto and intention as you would celebrate that individual, even if your win seems significantly smaller. That level of self-recognition and self-celebration encourages you to witness the value of your win, and continually work toward embodying further gains, too. Through this, you create a meaningful way to expand your mind power and embody the entirety of who you are through each new stage of your life.

CHAPTER 17
Create Healthy Habits

Habits are a practical aspect of life, are natural to your biology, and hold significant impact over your capacity to expand and reach into the depths of your mind power. From a biological and primal perspective, habits enable you to remove the conscious thought from routine experiences so you can conserve energy and invest it elsewhere. For example, if you always wake up, go to the bathroom, then start a pot of coffee, this becomes a habit, so your brain no longer has to invest energy into running your conscious mind through this loop. Instead, you simply do it on "autopilot."

Everything in our lives has been linked to one habit or another, unless you are particularly spontaneous in which case you still experience many things from a conscious perspective. Regardless of how spontaneous you may be, though, you will always find yourself engaging in a variety of habits, some of which benefit your life, and others that don't.

Creating healthy habits is a wonderful way to reinforce your sense of wellbeing, while also expanding space in your life for you to enjoy greater mind power. You can integrate healthy habits into your life by first understanding the habit loop, then understanding the essential tool of the habit pivot.

The habit loop was defined by psychologists as being a four-step cycle that reinforces itself, effectively wiring your brain with seemingly essential habits. The four steps are this: trigger, routine, reward, reinforce. Each time you experience these four steps, the habit becomes stronger and more deeply instilled in your mind. To break or change your habit, you must know how to use a habit pivot. The pivot means that your trigger, reward, and reinforcement stay the same, but your action changes. This is an essential piece of knowledge that allows you to quickly change any habit you engage in, effectively creating freedom from actions that cause issues in your life. For example, if you presently smoke, your trigger may be stress, smoking is the action, the reward is the freedom from stress, and the reinforcement is the dopamine rush you gained from following through. To pivot this habit, you will maintain your trigger (stress), your reward (relief from stress), and your reinforcement (the dopamine rush), but you will need to pivot your actions. You might pivot to chewing gum, running, or engaging in any other activity that allows you to eliminate stress. In doing so, you transform your habits using the path of least resistance.

Physically Embodying Healthy Habits

The power of your mind, and your capacity to live with activated kundalini energy, rely on you having a strong, healthy body. Embodying healthy habits like eating nutritional meals, staying hydrated, moving your body, sleeping properly, and taking care of any health considerations unique to you is important. Each person requires a different regimen as far as physical health goes, so it is valuable to spend time exploring your body, understanding your needs, and investing in creating a routine that works for you.

Though your physical wellness routine, and corresponding habits, may seem largely practical and even removed from your spiritual experience, you must realize the importance they carry with your spiritual well being. Without a sound body, you are unable to fully ground the power of spirit within you, as there is weakness and stress throughout your system. This does not mean you have to be free of illness; plenty of people live with illness and have a sound body that is capable of embodying the energy of spirit. You must uncover what wellness means for you and your unique body, and strive to live in the healthiest way possible. Do the things that allow your body to be at its strongest and thrive in its own way.

It can be easy to slip on habits that support our physical wellness, because the body is resilient. Despite not being adequately cared for, your body can still move you through many obstacles and allow you to achieve many things in life. You must never settle for a body that merely gets by, though. Create habits that allow your body to thrive, as this is the highest level of respect you can show yourself.

Healthy Habits for Your Limitless Mind

Like with physical habits, it can be easy to let your mental habits slip. Regardless of your wellness plan, your mind will run and will bring you forward through life. It can be easy to succumb to negativity bias, complaining, and complacency when you do not take adequate care of your mind. Many also find it easy to fall into victim patterns, people pleasing, and complete burnout because they engage in habits that are not healthy to their mind.

To tap into your limitless mind power and fully embody the power of life force energy, you must learn to take proper care of your mind. Healthy habits that nourish your mind involve stress-relieving habits, reading, pursuing personal growth, learning, engaging in puzzles, reinforcing your memory, and engaging in optimistic and positive thinking. The more you allow yourself to tap into the expansive capabilities of your mind and use them to your advantage, especially with problem-solving and gaining the most out of life, the stronger your mindset habits will be. Through this, you drastically improve your mind power.

Caring for Your Emotions With Healthy Habits

Your emotions tie into your mental habits, though they stand alone. While mental behaviors include things like self-talk, memory, and problem-solving, emotional behaviors include the actual creation, expression, and release of your emotions. Healthy emotional habits are designed to support your ability to intentionally choose your emotions, express them in a meaningful way, and release them when you are done with them. This expands your mind power by providing you with direct control over your emotional self and the ability to use your emotions to your advantage. Rather than being hijacked by your emotions, which is common when your primal brain takes control, you learn how to stimulate them and use them to your advantage. Emotions will still be spontaneously created through uncontrollable day to day experiences; however, you will have a significant advantage with navigating and expressing your emotions intentionally. You may also use them to impact intentional, meaningful change in your life.

Excellent habits involving emotional health include spending time investing in the creation of emotions you desire, developing self-awareness around your emotional experiences, and creating space for you to express and release your emotions intentionally. This is especially important if you frequently find yourself experiencing emotions at times where it may be inappropriate to express such emotions. Providing yourself adequate time to bring them back to the surface and work through them later is an excellent way to fully release them, so they no longer sit in your energy field, sabotaging your mind power and embodiment of spiritual energy.

Nurturing Your Spirit With Healthy Habits

Although your spirit is an intangible aspect of yourself, it plays a large role in your wellbeing. Embodying healthy habits that nurture your spirit is an empowering way to elevate the quality of your life. Many people neglect their spiritual well being entirely, largely based on the fact that they cannot see, touch, or experience their spirit in a tangible manner. This unfortunate approach leads to feelings of disconnect, isolation, and a lack of faith, which can significantly damage your self-confidence and self-esteem.

Creating healthy habits that nurture your spiritual well being enables you to experience the support, faith, and growth that come from being deeply connected. Excellent spiritual habits include reinforcing your faith, praying, meditating, connecting with your energy, calling on your energy, and relying on the guidance you receive. You also support your spiritual wellbeing and connection each time you take care of your physical, mental, and emotional wellbeing, as you create a sound foundation for your spiritual self to exist.

CHAPTER 18
Open Yourself Up To Change

Change is a beautiful, necessary aspect of life. Our modern perception of change is often delusional and even damaged. We see change as a necessity for economic growth or increased power, often using it as a tool to feed our ego and our materialistic gains. Our view of change implies we must always be in control of change and leading the changes in our lives head on. The idea of releasing control and allowing change to happen seems unnatural, illogical, and even risky as we fear that doing so could lead to us experiencing change in a negative way. Of course, change is inevitable and, despite our best efforts, is rarely housed within our control. Yes, you may influence the change in your life, yet you cannot directly control it. Adjusting your perspective of change, and opening yourself to the natural evolution of life, is necessary to your wellbeing and the embodiment of your mind power.

Embodying a Daily Kundalini Ritual

Kundalini is a powerful catalyst, aiding you in transforming everything in your life from the inside out. Embodying a daily kundalini ritual enables you to invoke, embody, and engage in the power of life force energy. As you work through your ritual, you invite in the energies that motivate transformation and inspire change in your life. Further, the actual embodiment of a daily kundalini ritual will likely be a change in and of itself, because you are now creating from a space of intention and energy.

Each time you engage in your kundalini ritual, make space for you to set an intention and use that intention to your advantage. Call in the guidance of your intuition, life force energy, and the gods and heavens to support you with navigating change, whether it be specific or in general. Allow yourself to embody that guidance and follow it faithfully, as it moves you through any changes you may face in a fluid, comfortable manner.

Opening Yourself Up to Change

Despite change being a necessary and inevitable part of life, you may struggle with the concept of change. Perhaps you are afraid of opening up to change, for fear of losing the comfort you have created for yourself. As humans, we equate comfort to safety, which means we have no need to fear our stability. In other words, we have no need to fear our ability to survive because we have secured our survival through safety and comfort. The idea of expanding beyond your comfort zone and embracing change is terrifying, as it means moving away from the safety and putting yourself "at risk."

Fortunately, our modern lives are rarely risky to the point of your survival being threatened, and the steps you take to expand beyond your comfort zone are unlikely to threaten you, either. By adjusting your perspective and realizing that change is valuable and meaningful, you create space for positive change to occur in your life.

An excellent perspective to embody when it comes to addressing change is the perspective of detached evolution. The idea that we can stay fixed in our comfort zones and remain comfortable, prevent change, or control change, leads to stress when we realize that change is inevitable and rarely controllable. Through the perspective of detached evolution, you release the need for everything to go your way, or for things to turn out as you plan them to. Instead, you lean into faith and trust everything to turn out positively, or at least in a way that you can adapt to.

Work With Change Intentionally

Despite the fact that you cannot control change, there are many things you can control within change itself. You can cause change, embrace change, and work with the natural flow of change to influence it to go your way. Though you may not be able to stimulate the exact changes you desire, you can encourage the outcome to be more favorable or closer to your preferences. Often, the result of change will always be something far more meaningful than what you originally intended anyway, as change is life's natural way of moving us through our earthly experiences.

Working with change intentionally can be done at three separate stages: the cause of change, the behavior of change, and the outcome of change. You may cause change by identifying areas in your life where change must occur and behaving differently in these areas. Showing up with different energy, attitude, and actions can motivate these areas of your life to be transformed entirely. It may take a while for change to sink in; however, the more you embody these changed behaviors within yourself, the greater the catalyst will become for the change you are affecting.

During the behavior of change, you may identify the changes that are occurring and work within them to influence them to work to your benefit. For example, let's say you are moving to a new house in a new city, which is a change you caused. You may not be able to control who you meet, what types of friendships you have, or how you fit into your new community; however, you can take action to encourage this to be a positive experience. By working in alignment with change, you keep yourself open to meeting the right people that add value to your life and support you with feeling a sense of belonging in your new community.

When you reach the outcome of change, you may work with it intentionally by accepting the outcome and discovering ways that you can use the outcome to your advantage. Perhaps it did not turn out as you expected, or it even turned out poorly. You can always pick up the pieces, adapt to the outcome, or effect further change if you are displeased with the way things turned out. Through these actions, you gain the ability to work in harmony with change, rather than push against it or live with a lack of peace due to your ever evolving circumstances.

Being the Most Adaptable Version of Yourself

Embracing change is easiest if you become the most adaptable version of yourself. Being adaptable means that, regardless of what happens in your life, you can adapt and experience the highest quality of life possible. This is a deeply peaceful space to exist in, as it enables you to embrace all aspects of life without pushing against them or clinging for things to stay the same.

Mindset is your most powerful weapon in adaptability, as it allows you to view things from a perspective of openness, willingness, and adaptiveness. The theory of detachment is especially helpful to your adaptability, as detachment allows you to release the need to cling to any specific state of being or experience. This way, as life naturally changes, you are able to accept and embrace all aspects of change. The more you allow yourself to embrace this perspective, the stronger your adaptability skills will become.

CHAPTER 19
Exercise The Power Of Creativity

Creativity carries a phenomenal impact on your capacity to embrace life force energy and expand your mind power. Everything in existence got there because of creativity, and the power of creativity has driven us to exponential heights. From creating technology to discovering language and expanding our self-awareness, creativity has enabled us to reach impressive heights as a society, and as a species.

Kundalini energy, and life force energy, both carry with them significant energies of creation. Moving that energy through you and into the world surrounding you is a phenomenal way to work with that energy and create more space for it in your life. As you continue to call on it and use it, it will continue to flow through you naturally and with more significant strength.

Through creation, you gain many values. Manifestation, invention, and experience are all empowered through the energy of creation. Moreover, you experience a deep connection to the present moment and an exhilarating state of flow that drastically impacts your overall sense of wellbeing.

Creativity Is at the Root of Manifesting

Manifesting is a skill everyone desires to improve in their lives, and it is one we all have the capacity to embody. As you awaken your kundalini and expand your mind power, you gain the capacity to tap into your infinite creative abilities and manifest anything you desire. People have been manifesting since the beginning of time, conjuring up images in their minds of the things and lives they desired and calling them in through phenomenal manifesting abilities. At the root of it all was the life force energy and their capacity to create.

To expand into your manifesting abilities, you must first call on the power of your imagination. You may find it easy to imagine all that you desire, or you may find you have to be patient and practice working within your imagination to expand your abilities. If you struggle with using your imagination, meditation is a great opportunity to expand your creative abilities and draw forth images of all you desire to your mind. It also helps to clear away any limiting beliefs by pretending that there are no caps and limitations to what you can attract into your life. This often feels entirely unnatural and even directly opposing everything you have learned in your life; however, manifesting and embracing the power of your imagination are your birthright. Everyone has the power to manifest, as we are all born with this natural power.

If you find you struggle with manifesting or expanding your mind power through creativity, it often helps to scale down what you seek to create. Rather than attempting to call in an entire lifestyle and massive goals from the start, consider looking at opportunities to manifest smaller things. Manifest the ability to visualize your desires in your mind or to call smaller things into your life, such as a certain symbol or experience you desire to have. Once you become fluent in calling forward these smaller experiences, manifesting larger desires becomes easier, because you become used to following your intuition and life force energies.

Unlocking the Power of Your Creativity

To fully unlock the power of creativity through kundalini, you must first tap into your kundalini energies. The farther you dive into your awakening and the activation of your life force energy, creativity naturally starts to emerge. Often, practitioners who dig deep into their journey find they suddenly have a desire to sing, paint, write, or engage in another creative outlet. At the root of each of our minds is a deep desire to create something, as a form of expression and an opportunity to explore the world and universe through alternate senses. Art has always been fundamental to our society, and our individual wellbeing, so it makes sense that we thrive when we call it into our lives.

If you desire to call on and engage the power of your creativity in a specific moment, it can be helpful to first engage in a kundalini yoga session. This way, you embody kundalini within your body, activate your life force energy, and open space for you to be influenced by the world around you. Throughout your session, you may find inspiration for something to create, or the momentum to work toward a creation you had already been inspired to take action on. Or, you might find that you need to rest in meditation following a session for several moments to call in the inspiration to create. Regardless, you will inevitably feel the energy of creation move through you, so long as you remain open and willing to receive it.

Understand that, upon activating your creative energies, you may not be good at whichever outlet you choose to engage in. At first, you will be a beginner like anyone else. However, you will rapidly uncover the independent essence of your creativity that makes your work unique to you. Further, you will discover that the urge you have to create provides you with a sense of momentum that keeps you working toward developing your greatness each day. This is how people become excellent at what they do.

Steps to Expand Your Creativity

Invoking life force energy to stimulate your creativity is an excellent way to tap into this power; however, there are other practical steps you can take toward developing your creativity expanding mind power, too. By taking practical action, you create space for the spiritual energy of creativity to root in and expand through you, effectively expanding your life force energy and your mind power.

One excellent way to expand your creativity is through collaboration. Being curious and collaborating with others enables you to open yourself up to learning from them, while also being inspired by the presence of their energy and the unique energy they manifest themselves, too. Together, you might discover that your collaboration itself presents a form of energy that triggers inspiration and motivates each of you to embrace and live in the energy of creativity.

Following your passion, or those loving urges you feel inside yourself is another excellent way to expand your creativity. When you do something you love, you have a deep hunger within you to continue pursuing that activity and learning more about it, which stimulates your momentum and the development of your creative energy.

If following others' or expanding into existing momentum does not do the trick, you can always focus on retreating, instead. Sometimes, unplugging, giving yourself time away, and taking a genuine break is plenty to inspire you with new creative energies. Rather than trying to force your existing routine, or the creation of anything, fully surrender to a break. Go for peaceful walks, take care of yourself, enjoy plenty of relaxation, and make time for calmness, and see if inspiration strikes during those peaceful moments. Often, it is within the stillness and silence of life that our greatest inspiration strikes, as we finally pause and relax long enough to give it the space it needs to manifest.

If that doesn't work, you can always stimulate your creativity through idea lists and the practice of choosing the worst idea possible. Start by taking your idea notebook and writing down every idea you have, no matter how significant or insignificant it is. Do not confine yourself around what you ought to create, either. Write down everything from inventions and story ideas to paintings and artwork you can create, and keep going until you genuinely run out of ideas. Then, pick the worst idea from your book and begin taking action on that idea. Often, following the worst idea and genuinely putting the plan in action can motivate you to uncover a great idea, which will inspire you to design something new and impressive.

Integrating Creativity Into Your Everyday Life

Compartmentalizing your life is a sure way to confuse yourself and lose out on the value of a life that is orchestrated to be an overall experience. Far too often, people want to segregate the different areas of their lives as an opportunity to force each of these categories into a small, neat box. Unfortunately, you cannot expand in one area of your life without expanding in all, and if you shrink in one area of life, you will experience shrinkage in all areas, too. Separating everything into categories prevents you from harmonizing your experience and expression and embracing the many values life has to offer.

Rather than segregating your life into different categories, learn to view your entire life as a canvas, and integrate creativity into everything you do. Discover how you can creatively apply lessons from one area of your life to all areas of your life, stay hungry enough to expand in every way possible, and put effort into creating a life that fulfills you overall. Through this, your entire life becomes a canvas that you get to use to create the life you desire.

Do everything with intention and creativity, looking for ways to bring self-expression and meaning into each step. Whether it be turning your nightly hygiene routine into a meaningful ritual, or the way you eat into a form of self-expression, discover how to overturn mundane tasks with creativity. Integrating creativity into all areas of your life enables you to engage in the energy of life and reap as much joy from it as you possibly can.

If you desire to embrace the energy of creativity for the power of manifestation, this is an excellent opportunity to reach that stage, too. With each task you engage in, creatively integrate elements of your desires into it. Visualize yourself pursuing your dreams, see yourself experiencing it from an expanded state of awareness, and behave as though you have already created the experiences of your dreams. Through this, you expand your creativity through imagination and playing pretend, while also using energy to create the life you desire in every way possible. This is how you gain the opportunity to become the most creative person possible, while enjoying the energy of authentic self-expression.

CONCLUSION

Congratulations on reading *Kundalini*! This book was intended to show you the many ways you can integrate kundalini into your everyday life so you can live from an expanded point of consciousness and perception. Awakening kundalini energy is about far more than just following the mainstream trends or a journey your friend invited you on that you unknowingly agreed to. Kundalini is a personal journey that is intended to support you with accessing the entirety of your energy so you can activate it and use it in your everyday life. Life is significantly more meaningful and enjoyable when you embrace it with your maximum energy, and continue to expand into your energy so you can experience more out of life.

I hope reading this book has encouraged you to discover just how impactful a kundalini awakening is, and how extensively this energy can transform your life. Beyond connecting you to abundant life force energy, it can also provide you with the capacity to approach life from an entirely unique perspective. Engaging in life from this grounded, empowering angle enables you to gain everything that life has to offer, while also balancing your energies so you can experience greater enlightenment.

Enlightenment and the process of awakening is, genuinely, a never ending journey. So long as you are alive on earth, you have the potential to continually expand your energy and mind power. If you desire full enlightenment and the experience of the heavens and gods, it is worth it to continue to explore how this energy can be integrated into your life. Not only will this expand your enlightenment, but it also deepens the joy and fulfillment you gain from life itself.

After reading this book, it is worth it to continue studying the nature of kundalini and the many ways you can integrate this energy into your life. Investing in study is a wonderful way to expand your perspective, gain insight into how you can integrate life force energy into your earthly experience, and increase the value you gain from life itself. It also allows you to carefully remove yourself from the earthly experiences of suffering, providing you with the opportunity to heal and experience greater success in your life.

If you have not already, I encourage you to integrate a daily kundalini routine into your life, which enables you to tap into your life force energy and experience the depths of it. As you continue to tap in, your understanding of kundalini and life force energy will expand, offering you greater insight into the energy of life and the purpose of your life.

Before you go, I ask that you please take a moment to review *Kundalini* on Amazon. Your honest feedback would be greatly appreciated, as it provides others' with the opportunity to uncover the value to be gained from this book.

Thank you, and best of luck with your awakening and the expansion of your mind power!

DESCRIPTION

Kundalini energy is an expansive, empowering energy that will entirely transform your life from the inside out. Discover how kundalini energy can be integrated into your everyday life and experience the value of your higher capabilities by tapping into your expanded mind power. In *Kundalini,* we will discuss how you can realize your highest potential and experience the magnitude of life itself.

In this book, you will discover powerful, practical measures for integrating kundalini into your life experience, while also using it to create the life of your dreams. Be aware, though – the life of your dreams is unlikely to be the one you originally imagined it would be. Upon activating your kundalini energies, you will likely discover that you trade your materialistic desires for spiritual gains or personal growth, all of which are capable of providing you with an abundance of fulfillment and joy.

The primary topics we cover in this book include the physical and spiritual methods for approaching mind power and expanding your potential. Through reading this book, you will discover everything you need to practically and spiritually embrace the life you desire.

Physically, we will discuss how movement, diet, and practical self-care measures can provide you with a solid foundation to root your life force energy into. The more you care for your body, the stronger your spiritual integration can become, and the more you gain from this energy.

Spiritually, we will discuss how you can engage in meaningful rituals that expand your capacity to call in life force energy and work with it intentionally. Through this approach, you gain the capacity to co-create your life in a way that serves your highest good.

The specific topics we cover in *Kundalini* include:

- What mind power is, and how it is affected by physical and spiritual experiences

- Why food affects your energy and how to consume an energy balancing and expanding diet with Ayurveda
- The value of kundalini yoga and how you can integrate this into your daily life
- How relationships affect mind power and the necessary steps to expanding your energy through lovingly detached relationships
- The number one killer of mind power, and how you can spot and eliminate it from your life
- Which mindsets empower your mind power and provide you with growth opportunities
- Why you must deepen your sense of self and how this improves your life experience
- The value of tapping into your problem-solving abilities so you can enjoy the natural abilities of your mind
- Why you need to engage in an ego death, and how to choose happiness
- The theory of mirrors and why everyone around you is a mirror for you
- How to invoke the energy of creativity and use it to your advantage
- And more!

Kundalini is the ultimate go-to guide for anyone that wishes to expand their mind power and embrace the value of kundalini in their everyday life. Buy your copy today and discover how you can embody kundalini and life force energy practically!

www.ingramcontent.com/pod-product-compliance
Lightning Source LLC
Chambersburg PA
CBHW081347070526
44578CB00005B/754